Cottonclads!

The Battle of Galveston
and the Defense of the Texas Coast

CIVIL WAR CAMPAIGNS AND COMMANDERS SERIES

Under the General Editorship of Grady McWhiney

PUBLISHED

Cottonclads!
The Battle of Galveston and the Defense of the Texas Coast

Donald S. Frazier

Under the General Editorship of Grady McWhiney

RYAN PLACE PUBLISHERS
FORT WORTH   BOULDER

Cataloging-in-Publication Data

Frazier, Donald S. (Donald Shaw), 1965—
    Cottonclads!; the Battle of Galveston and the defense of the
Texas coast / Donald S. Frazier: under the general editorship of
Grady McWhiney.
        p. cm. — (Civil War campaigns and commanders)
        Includes bibliographical references and index.
        ISBN 1-886661-09-X (pbk)

    1. Galveston, Battle of, 1863. I. McWhiney, Grady. II. Title.
III. Series.
        E474.1.F739 1996
        973.7'33—dc20   95–51436
                                                                         CIP

2730 Fifth Avenue
Fort Worth, Texas 76110

ISBN 1-886661-09-X
10 9 8 7 6 5 4 3 2 1

Book Designed by Rosenbohm Design Group

All inquiries regarding volume purchases of this book should be
addressed to Ryan Place Publishers, Inc., 2525 Arapahoe Avenue,
Suite E4-231, Boulder, CO 80302-6720.

SAN: 298-6779

A Note on the Series

Few segments of America's past excite more interest than Civil War battles and leaders. This ongoing series of brief, lively, and authoritative books–*Civil War Campaigns and Commanders*–salutes this passion with inexpensive and accurate accounts that are readable in a sitting. Each volume, separate and complete in itself, nevertheless conveys the agony, glory, death, and wreckage that defined America's greatest tragedy.

In this series, designed for Civil War enthusiasts as well as the newly recruited, emphasis is on telling good stories. Photographs and biographical sketches enhance the narrative of each book, and maps depict events as they happened. Sound history is meshed with the dramatic in a format that is just lengthy enough to inform and yet satisfy.

Grady McWhiney
General Editor

CONTENTS

The brief biographies accompanying the photographs were written by Grady McWhiney and David Coffey.

CAMPAIGNS AND COMMANDERS SERIES

Map Key

Geography

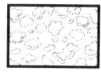 Trees

 Marsh

 Fields

 Strategic Elevations

 Rivers

Tactical Elevations

 Fords

 Orchards

Political Boundaries

Human Construction

 Bridges

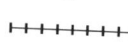 Railroads

 Tactical Towns

Strategic Towns

Buildings

Church

Roads

Military

 Union Infantry

 Confederate Infantry

 Cavalry

 Artillery

Headquarters

Encampments

Fortifications

Permanant Works

Hasty Works

Obstructions

 Engagements

 Warships

Gunboats

Casemate Ironclad

Monitor

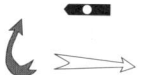 Tactical Movements

 Strategic Movements

Maps by
Donald S. Frazier, Ph.D.
Abilene, Texas

MAPS AND DIAGRAMS

PHOTOGRAPHS AND ILLUSTRATIONS

Cottonclads!

The Battle of Galveston
and the Defense of the Texas Coast

1
THE ANACONDA

Winfield Scott, the aged and wizened veteran of most of America's wars, faced his biggest challenge in 1861. The nation looked to the seventy-five-year-old warrior for an answer: How could the Union be saved? Scott believed that outright invasion of the seceded states would be a disaster. Instead, he drew upon his understanding of Americans—Southerners in particular—and developed what he thought was a sensible, and safe, plan.

As by the constrictions of an anaconda, he argued, the Confederacy could be isolated and strangled into submission. Time, he believed, was a Union ally. The U.S. Navy, by imposing a tight blockade on the Southern coast, would slowly stop the economic engine that, Scott figured, was driving the secession movement. An associated campaign to capture the Mississippi would split the separatist nation in two, weakening it further. As Southerners saw their financial well-being jeopardized, they would ultimately give up and return to the Union. It might take several years, but Scott's plan wouldn't require much bloodshed. It would require, however, hundreds of ships.

President Abraham Lincoln was only partially convinced. He liked most of the tenets of Scott's plan, but realized several weaknesses. The U.S. Navy counted only fifty commissioned vessels, far fewer than would be needed to watch 3,500 miles of Southern coastline. In addition, Lincoln led a coalition government, an odd combination of radicals and moderates. The radicals in his government and his constituency demanded more action than Scott's war of constriction. Even so, Lincoln did declare a blockade of the seceded states, in effect on April 19, 1861, at the same time that he made plans for a major land war.

David Glasgow Farragut: born Tennessee 1801; after moving with his family to New Orleans, Farragut came under the guardianship of Captain David Porter; in 1810, at not yet ten years of age, he was appointed midshipman in the U.S. Navy; the following year he joined Porter's crew aboard the frigate *Essex*; serving in the Pacific during the War of 1812, he was appointed prize master of a captured British vessel; Farragut was actively engaged during Porter's defeat by two British warships at Valparaiso; taken prisoner, he was exchanged in November 1814; his next five years were spent on duty mostly in the Mediterranean; he studied in Tunis and, in 1825, became a lieutenant; thereafter he saw a variety of duties in the Gulf of Mexico and the south Atlantic; in 1841 he was promoted to commander and, the following year, took command of the sloop *Decatur*; he was largely left out of the action during the Mexican War; given command of the sloop *Saratoga*, he arrived too late to participate in the capture of Vera Cruz; following another period of varied assignments, during which he received promotion to captain, he was, at the outbreak of the Civil War, awaiting orders at his home in Norfolk, Virginia;

By the end of that first year of war, Union troops had invaded the South while the navy sought to plug the gaps in its imperfect blockade. Armies grew upon the land, fought major battles, and initiated a campaign to capture the Mississippi. In addition, a brown water navy arose from Western river ports to aid the army in its labors. On the ocean, Yankee tars commandeered seemingly everything afloat to enforce the blockade and naval agents enlisted New York ferryboats, clipper ships, and anything else that could carry a gun. These converted civilians were far from beautiful, but they served their purpose. As these ships and scows captured Confederate runners, the navy dragooned the prize vessels as well into the service of the United States.

with Virginia's secession, he moved his family to New York; as a Southerner, he was initially viewed with suspicion—his only assignment in 1861 being on a retirement board; in January 1862 he was given command of the West Gulf Blockading Squadron, with the mission of capturing New Orleans; in April 1862 he did just that; with the bulk of his fleet he ran past Forts Jackson and St. Philip and captured the defenseless city in what may have been the most decisive single action of the war—one from which the Confederate government could not rebound; for this he was promoted to rear admiral; thereafter he moved up the Mississippi and, in July 1862, fought his way past Vicksburg before returning to the Gulf of Mexico; he again ascended the Mississippi to attack Port Hudson in March 1863; in July of that year he returned to New York and received a hero's welcome; he returned to the Gulf in January 1864 to begin operations against Mobile; in August 1864 his fleet engaged the Confederate Forts Morgan and Gaines; aboard his flagship *Hartford*, Farragut is reported to have exclaimed "Damn the torpedoes, full speed ahead" as he led the fleet past the forts and through a mine field—both forts capitulated by month's end; in December, suffering from poor health, he again returned to New York, where the citizens presented him with $50,000 with which to purchase a house there; he also received promotion to vice admiral; he returned to duty in the waning moments of the conflict and was among the first Federal officers to enter Richmond after its fall; in July 1866 he became the first full admiral in the nation's history; after the war he commanded the European Squadron; Admiral Farragut died at Portsmouth, New Hampshire, in 1870, still on active duty in his sixtieth year of service to the U.S. Navy.

Unable to completely seal off the Confederacy by simply patrolling its coastal waters with this menagerie of home–grown and captured ships, the navy changed strategy. Amphibious operations seized key inlets and ports. Infantry would serve the purposes of the blockade by garrisoning these Union enclaves. The captured areas would in turn serve as forward bases for other naval operations in the area. This new tack proved successful among the peninsulas of Virginia and the coastal islands of the Carolinas, and became doctrine for the rest of the war.

New Orleans held the keys to the Anaconda Plan. Like a hinge joining the blockade to the land-based war effort on the Mississippi, the Crescent City occupied perhaps the most strategic point in North America. Union planners wasted little time in mounting a major campaign to capture that city. In April 1862, after a year of war, New Orleans fell to Union forces under Admiral David G. Farragut and General Benjamin Butler.

While Butler moved his troops into position to squash any remaining Rebel resistance near New Orleans, Admiral David Farragut moved with alacrity to seize control of the Mississippi. On May 9, Union sailors and marines from the U.S.S. *Iroquois* captured Baton Rouge without a shot, taking possession of the U.S. arsenal and barracks. Farragut, the bulk of his fleet, and transports loaded with 1,500 infantrymen, followed from New Orleans to secure the town. By May 13, Farragut's fleet had scouted northward, capturing Natchez, Mississippi. Arriving before Vicksburg four days later, the Union forces demanded the town's surrender, hoping to capture that key position before Confederates could occupy its strategic heights.

Rebel Columbiads and other artillery disappointed the Union sailors, however. Sensing the emergency, all Confederate troops that had been evacuated from New Orleans, along with those in garrison in various places in

Mississippi, had rushed to occupy Vicksburg and to man a dozen heavy guns overlooking the river. Thwarted, Farragut and most of his fleet returned to Baton Rouge to await developments.

Foiled on the Mississippi, Farragut instead turned his attention back to blockade duties, and to extending control of the navy into the western Gulf of Mexico. Regular naval vessels accompanied by a collection of makeshift warships soon began implementing his plan of closing all of the odd inlets and bays in Louisiana and Texas. Although Union ships had begun patrolling the coast there in 1861, that portion of the blockade leaked badly. Farragut decided to plug the holes.

The most important of the Texas ports, by far, were Sabine Pass, Galveston, and Brazos Santiago at the mouth of the Rio Grande. The last, however, lay too far away from Union supply and repair facilities at New Orleans, and appeared well defended. The other two possessed few defenses but sported

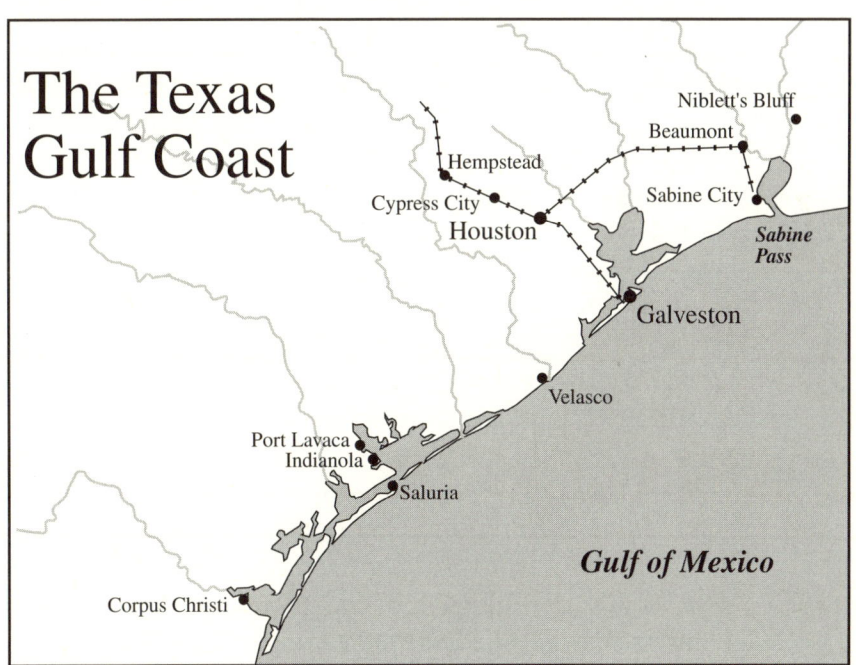

the best port facilities in the state. Dozens of small blockade runners sought refuge in their shallow waters, and carried on a lively trade with Mexico and the Caribbean.

Secondary targets of more marginal utility also lined the coast. Velasco, at the mouth of the Brazos and near the mouth of the San Bernard, offered a poor anchorage and was plagued by sand bars but housed a swarm of small light draft vessels waiting for favorable tides and winds to make a dash to Mexico. Matagorda Bay, the approach to the port towns of Saluria, Indianola and Port Lavaca, was shallow and treacherous to pilots unfamiliar with it. Corpus Christi, sheltered by Mustang Island, would one day be an excellent port, but in 1862 still lay on the frontier far away from the settled portion of the state, and with correspondingly undeveloped facilities.

Both Sabine Pass and Galveston benefited from a decent prewar volume of traffic that had led to improved channels and port facilities. From Farragut's standpoint, too, they lay within easy reach of supplies and repairs at New Orleans. Galveston held a special appeal to the admiral for a variety of reasons. Galveston was the largest city in Texas and its capture would be a severe blow to Texas morale. In addition, the city was on an island, giving the advantage to the legless navy. With little effort, Farragut reasoned, the blockade could be swiftly and strictly enforced on the coast of Texas with the capture of Galveston. Its port facilities would provide the Union with a forward base to operate against other targets farther down the coast.

Union vessels probed the Texas coastal defenses by attacking Corpus Christi first. In mid-August 1862, a flotilla composed of the twin-masted, fore-and-aft-rigged sailing schooners U.S.S. *Corypheus*, U.S.S. *Reindeer*, the small sailing sloop U.S.S. *Belle Italia*, the square-rigged bark U.S.S. *Arthur*, and the small steamer U.S.S. *Sachem*, destroyed five commercial boats of various sizes in the bay and surrounding waters. Although stymied by the garrison of Corpus Christi after a two-day artillery duel, the navy continued making prizes of other blockade runners for weeks. This partial success would whet the appetite of the U.S. Navy.

These victories came as a surprise to most involved. The few second-rate Union ships had operated with ease against the unprepared coast, and had exceeded expectations. While never totally destroying the Rebel positions or capturing the Texas ports, Union sailors and marines had spread a good deal of panic through the state.

This good news was indeed welcome to Farragut, still smarting from the frustrations of the Mississippi. Not surprisingly, he decided to reinforce success, detaching a large portion of his naval assets to operations against Texas. Within a few months, he hoped, even this far corner of the Confederacy would feel the coils of the anaconda.

2
THE WEST GULF
BLOCKADING SQUADRON

The eastern horizon was slowly turning gray on September 24, 1862, as two small schooners silently glided into Sabine Pass, Texas. Slowly, deliberately, they tacked into position more than two and a half miles away from a small earthwork flying the Stars and Bars of the Confederate States. As the Union blue jackets steered their vessels with wind and tide, Texan gunners stood to their guns and watched the nimble sailing craft maneuver. As the bright orange sun crested the east in a blaze of light, the Federal ships slowed their progress, the Stars and Stripes flowing fitfully in a moderate breeze.

The Confederates on shore saw the flash and smoke first, then heard the booming pop carry across the water as the whir of solid shot furrowed the air toward their position. A white geyser of water and a few tell-tale skips showed that the twelve-pound shot had fallen short. Next, a deeper, growling rumble announced the launching of the first of three massive mortar rounds, each falling progressively nearer the Texans.

To most of the untried gunners in the muddy fort, this was the first time anyone had deliberately tried to kill them. Exhilarated by this harmless introduction to war, the Texans, mostly older twenty-year-olds from the surrounding region, gamely replied. Their mismatched collection of long and short ranged 32-pounders bucked and lurched backwards as crews strained for the range of the offending vessels. Their shots,

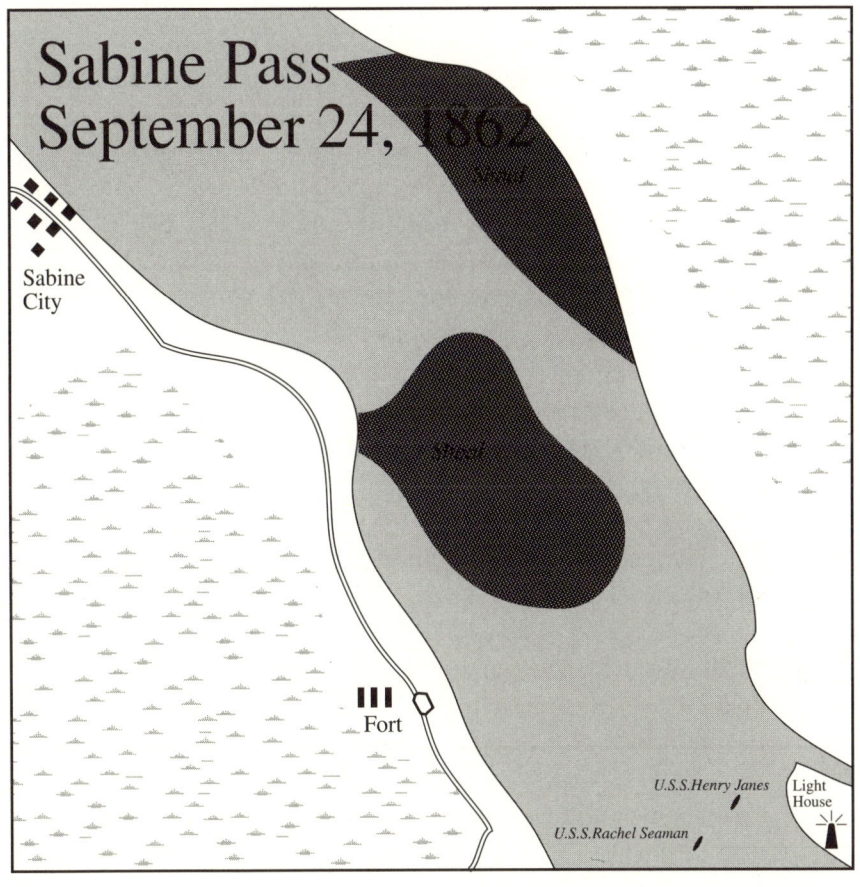

too, smacked the water. After exchanging nearly a dozen rounds, both sides fell silent—each out of range of the other. The rest of the day, the Texans watched as the Union crews, their ships' boats in advance, carried kedging anchors to the length of their cables, then dropped them to the ocean floor. Crews aboard the ships then strained at their anchor cables, dragging their warships closer toward shore for a better shot. The Union vessels were the schooner U.S.S. *Rachel Seaman* and the mortar boat U.S.S. *Henry Janes*, their crews under orders to reduce the offending Rebel work or to drive the garrison from its guns.

After a hard day of pulling rope by the Union crews, the gunners on both sides renewed the duel at 5 P.M. Within minutes, the seemingly playful salutes of the morning were replaced by firing in deadly earnest. High-trajectory mortar rounds spiraled over and through the Texan positions, trailing a sparking, smoky tail. Some rounds burst overhead; others landed solidly in the fort, showering the Rebels with mud and debris. The 12-pounder rifle of the *Rachel Seaman* sent shot zipping into and past the fort. Despite the noise of explosions and the impact of iron on mud—not to mention the distractions of white-hot shell fragments spinning through the air— none of the Texans were hit. Gamely serving their guns, the thirty Confederates soon discovered that, despite their best efforts, their rounds still fell short by a few hundred yards of the enemy ships. Even so, the men continued trying until their officers restrained them from fruitlessly wasting ammunition. Without a way to reply, some of the more reckless clambered up the parapet and waved their hats in defiance at the vessels in the distance. The bombardment lasted the rest of the afternoon, with increasing effect. Unable to destroy the Texan position by nightfall, the Union ships eventually forced its gamecock garrison to seek cover. As dusk lengthened, the two Union schooners ceased firing and slipped back toward the Gulf of Mexico.

Inside the Confederate works, Major Josephus S. Irvine, Texas Revolution veteran and commander of the post at Sabine Pass, and Captain K.D. Keith of Company B, 1st Texas Heavy Artillery, debated the morrow's course of action. Clearly the enemy had the advantage in artillery, having tossed light rifle shells into the Rebel works with impunity. The mortar, too, provided cause for alarm. Without an effective means of responding to the Union naval threat, resistance appeared futile.

Near midnight, reinforcements interrupted the two officers' gloomy deliberations as twenty-six infantrymen from Company E of Ashley Spaight's Texas Battalion arrived under the command of Captain G. W. O'Bryan. While encouraging the addled garrison, these newcomers did not change the equation. Besides the threat of bombardment, all understood that this meager outpost was vulnerable to being cut off as well—if the Union vessels passed the battery, moved up into the bay known as Sabine Lake, and landed troops. With enemy soldiers to the north, the garrison would have to evacuate via the only other route—the beach road toward Galveston. Not only would this circuitous path keep the evacuated garrison out of the war for several days, but the troops would be vulnerable to bombardment from the Gulf. After a few minutes of debate, the consensus appeared to be in favor of immediate evacuation. Major Irvine ordered his fort abandoned. That night, Captain Keith's Texans spiked their artillery and destroyed any public property that could not be carried away. After falling in with Captain O'Bryan's footsore infantry, the Confederates left their fort behind.

The next morning, the Union ships arrived back on station and discovered quickly that they had in fact silenced the Texan fort. After landing a detachment to investigate the smoldering ruins, Acting Master Frederick Crocker led the *Rachel Seaman* up Sabine Lake to further probe Rebel resolve in the area. Within days, Union shore parties from these and other ships including the U.S.S. *Kensington* had raided ashore to within a few miles of Beaumont, beginning a cycle of skirmishing with the Texas defenders that lasted for months. Soon, the key bridge on the railroad leading to Sabine Pass lay in ashes, as did the town of Sabine City and most of the buildings along the waterfront.

Southern engineers sensed the emergency and ordered obstructions to be set in the mouths of the Neches and Sabine Rivers to avoid Union "depredations up those streams." When news reached the Confederates that enemy naval officers had attempted to purchase beef from citizens, Rebel horsemen ran all of the livestock in the vicinity deep into the thickets of the interior. On occasion, Texans would ambush the Union landing parties or snipe at their ships, usually without significant effect.

Without adequate U.S. forces to secure shore positions, and with Texan resistance stiffening, a stalemate developed. At the

Frederick Crocker: born Massachusetts 1821; became a whaler during his youth; when the Civil War began, he offered his ship, the passenger steamer *R.R. Cuyler*, and his services to the Union; appointed an acting master in 1861, he resigned six months later, but was then reappointed in 1862, and given command of the U.S.S.

Kensington and thereafter promoted to the rank of acting volunteer lieutenant "for gallant conduct"; nearly six feet tall, with blue eyes, and a fair complexion, Crocker weighed 180 pounds; in 1863, while in command of the gunboat *Clifton* and other naval forces at the Battle of Sabine Pass, he was captured by Confederates and remained a prisoner of war until 1865; after a leave of absence, Crocker was appointed an acting volunteer lieutenant commander "for faithful and meritorious services" during the rebellion, and was honorably discharged from the navy; between 1876 and 1886, he served President Grant's administration as U.S. consul in Montevideo, Uruguay, where Crocker died and was buried in 1911.

same time, a yellow fever epidemic ran through the population on that portion of the coast. Faced with the twin dangers— muskets and microbes—The U.S. Navy broke the deadlock by choosing the safest course, opting against a close blockade of Sabine Pass and its environs. Accordingly, officers ordered their ships out of the shallow coastal waters and back into the Gulf of Mexico. Back in safer surroundings, and joined by the recently captured *Velocity*, Federal cannon kept this once active hideaway for blockade runners closed, occasionally venturing into Sabine Lake to spy on Rebel activities.

The fight at Sabine Pass, however, confirmed the principal weakness in Farragut's plan. The U.S. Navy seemed to have plenty of ships, and weekly augmented the number with captured Rebel blockade runners. This increase in the number of ships, however, served to thin out the number of sailors per vessel. The ships on station, as a result, had few crewmen to spare for shore parties and raiding; neither were there marines in any number. Farragut's captains would have made good use of any available infantry, but it, too, was in short supply. General Butler had marshaled all available forces in the lower Mississippi, and indeed had few to spare. With plenty of ships, but few men, the Navy found itself embarrassed to maintain any gains it made on shore.

The Confederates had also learned some lessons. While maintaining an abundance of men, they counted no warships worthy of the name in the Texas coastal waters. Their shore batteries were few and inadequate and were easy prey to well–handled enemy ships. The advantage and initiative, so it seemed, lay with the highly mobile Federals who could raid and retreat before the Texans could react. The Texans had constituted a mounted shore patrol to report and resist such Union tactics, but results had been thus far disappointing. Any successful defense of the region would come only after an adequate squadron of gunboats could be constructed to supplement the troops on shore.

In many ways, the equation was one of evolution and adaptation. The Union Navy needed to grow legs, while the Confederates needed to grow fins.

The fighting at Sabine Pass also proved Farragut's suspicions concerning the value of this and other Texas coast enclaves. When naval reinforcements arrived on station, the new Union observers commented on the significance of the place, and marveled that more aggressive efforts had not been made against it. "The importance of Sabine Pass to the Rebels appears to have been entirely underrated by us," an officer aboard the U.S.S. *Kensington* wrote to Admiral Farragut. "The quantity of goods of all kinds, and munitions of war that have been run in here has been enormous, and large quantities of cotton have been exported." In an ominous tone, the officer also noted the still lethal force lurking in the brown waters of Sabine Lake. "There are now lying above at least eight steamers and six schooners, large

William B. Renshaw: born New York 1816; Renshaw entered the U.S. Navy as a midshipman in 1831, becoming passed midshipman in 1837; after service at the New York Navy Yard, he was elevated to lieutenant in September 1841; at the outbreak of the Civil War he was promoted to commander and assigned to the

Ordnance Bureau in Washington, D.C.; transferred to the steamer *Westfield*, Renshaw took part in Admiral David G. Farragut's July 1862 attack on the Confederate ironclad *Arkansas* in the Mississippi below Vicksburg; promoted to commodore and given command of the gunboat flotilla investing Galveston, he captured that port with little opposition in October 1862; during the Confederate recapture of Galveston on 1 January 1863 the *Westfield* ran aground; he resolved to destroy his flagship, which contained large stocks of ammunition and powder, but the ship exploded prematurely, killing Commodore Renshaw and much of his crew; the Federals then abandoned the fight, leaving Galveston once again in Confederate hands.

quantities of cotton, and quite a force of troops."

Even so, the easy success of the Union ships at Sabine Pass gave Farragut reason to be optimistic as he planned his next move. Texans, too, he reasoned, should see the full face of war. He ordered Commander William Renshaw to lead four powerful gunboats, U.S.S. *Westfield, Clifton, Harriet Lane*, and *Owasco* deeper into the western Gulf to see what could be done about capturing Galveston.

The Confederates faced a crisis as the requirements of defense taxed Texan ingenuity along their four hundred-mile coastline. The four guns at Sabine Pass—now lost—constituted a major part of the Texan ordnance. Three batteries, 24- and 32-pounders, protected the Matagorda Bay and Corpus Christi vicinity.

Galveston had at one time stood the best guarded. Three mutually supporting batteries, positioned on Bolivar Point, Fort Point, and Pelican Spit, swept the channel and bay while a battery at San Luis Pass at the southwestern tip of the island closed that approach. Most of the guns emplaced were 24- and 32-pounders, but William Pitt Ballinger, one of the city's leading citizens, had also shepherded an eight-inch and ten-inch army Columbiad from east of the Mississippi to stiffen the Galveston defenses. General Paul O. Hébert, Confederate commander in Texas, did not believe that these few batteries could defend the city and in early 1862 had ordered all of the guns removed to the mainland. A fort built on Virginia Point would be the new line of defense for the state. Galveston, and its residents, lay abandoned on their island. The political storm that he created led to indecision and bad compromises that divided the Confederate cannons out into small parcels, each incapable of doing more than soothing citizens' anxieties. By the fall of 1862, Texan guns remained dispersed and exposed along Galveston Bay.

Commander, now Commodore, Renshaw arrived off Galveston on October 4 and decided to ask for the surrender of the city before shooting his way in. At daybreak on October 5, 1862, the commodore ordered the U.S.S. *Harriet Lane* under the command of Commander J. M. Wainwright to pass over the bar into Galveston Bay with a flag of truce. A shot from the ten-inch Columbiad on Fort Point at the tip of Galveston Island answered the ship's advance. The *Harriet Lane* dropped anchor and signaled for a boat from shore; after waiting impatiently, Commander Wainwright sent executive officer Lieutenant Commander Edward Lea ashore in his own boat. The Confederates were unhappy to see the Union officers, and hurried them back to their ship after a terse interview. Wainwright, again left waiting, grew stormy as he spied a small Confederate boat, flying a Rebel flag and not a flag of truce, slowly and clumsily making its way from shore. After watching the craft creep forward, the Union officer preemptively ordered his anchors weighed and turned his vessel about, deciding that

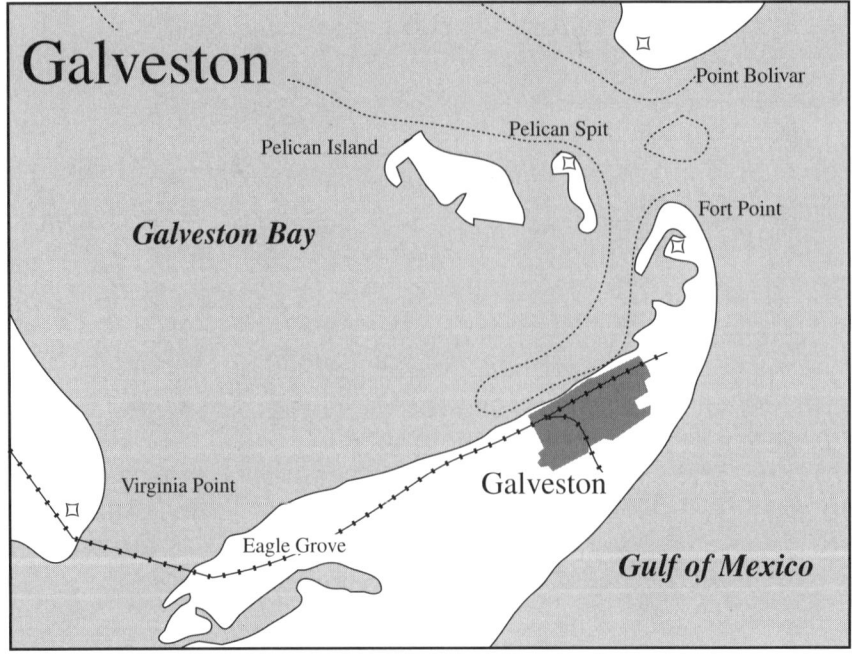

Galveston

Point Bolivar

Pelican Spit

Pelican Island

Galveston Bay

Fort Point

Virginia Point

Galveston

Eagle Grove

Gulf of Mexico

the Texans were bluffing, and probably stalling.

Daylight was waning, and the Federals realized that they had to act or give the Texans the nighttime to dig in. Renshaw, perplexed by Wainwright's report of the events near shore, decided to bring the whole squadron, including the just arrived mortar schooner *Henry Janes*, over the bar, running the Fort Point battery and gobbling up the Confederate boat en route. Before the Union ships could close with the enemy skiff, however, the gun on Fort Point opened fire. As the Rebel launch

Jonathan M. Wainwright: born New York 1821; at sixteen years of age Wainwright entered the U.S. Navy as a midshipman; he served aboard several vessels in the East and West Indies and participated in surveying activities in Chesapeake Bay; promoted to passed midshipman in June 1843, he was stationed at Washington, D.C., before again taking to the seas; after gaining promotion to lieutenant in September 1850, Wainwright sailed aboard the *San Jacinto* for duty in the Mediterranean; thereafter he served on the soon-to-be-famous *Merrimack* (1856–1857) and the *Saratoga*; following the outbreak of the Civil War, he was assigned to the *Minnesota* in the Atlantic Squadron; promoted to commander in January 1862, he took charge of the *Harriet Lane*, the flagship of the West Gulf Squadron's mortar flotilla; in February he captured the Confederate *Joanna Ward* off Florida's Gulf Coast; in April 1862 Wainwright played a conspicuous role in the reduction of Forts Jackson and St. Philip during the Federal capture of New Orleans; after further service on the Mississippi, Wainwright participated in the October 1862 capture of Galveston; on 1 January 1863, as Confederate  forces recaptured the Texas port, the *Harriet Lane* came under attack by two rebel vessels, the *Bayou City* and *Neptune*, and, in a fierce battle the *Harriet Lane* was boarded; already riddled with bullets, Commander Wainwright was killed by a shot through the head as he defended his ship. He was the grandfather of World War Two hero and Medal of Honor recipient General Jonathan Wainwright.

sprinted for home, Renshaw's blue jackets returned the Texan fire with a vengeance, a shell from the *Owasco* bursting just over the Rebel battery. The Texan gunners, men of the 1st Texas Heavy Artillery, fled from the combined weight of some twenty navy guns. Other rounds dismounted the Rebel gun, one shot striking it full on the muzzle. The ships then proceeded into the harbor under the ineffective fire of a pair of 24-pounders nearer town.

The Federals now moved boldly to finish their conquest. Renshaw anchored his ships near the city, again hoisting a white flag as the firing fell silent. While the cables slipped into the water, the Rebels responded by sending their boat back out, bearing army officers to confer with Renshaw. The Union sailor demanded the unconditional surrender of the city. After much posturing on both sides, with each accusing the other of violating a flag of truce, each side agreed to an armistice. Renshaw granted the Confederate authorities four days to remove women, children, and foreigners from the town, after which time he would take the city, by force if necessary.

With their heaviest gun lying in a heap on Fort Point, the Confederate authorities realized their cause as hopeless, and ordered Galveston evacuated. For four days, usually under cover of darkness, the Rebels removed anything of military importance, destroying materiel they could not transport. By the evening of October 8, just two companies of infantry remained at Eagle Grove, the island end of the railroad cause-way leading to Virginia Point and the mainland.

On October 9, 1862, the Civil War came to Texas. The once remote enemy sat anchored in Galveston Bay: Union warships were about to seize the state's largest city, and although this was not a grand showing by a large force, Farragut's Yankees had come to stay. A few bystanders nervously watched as a squad of U.S. Marines disembarked from their launch, climbed up the ladder at Kuhn's Wharf, and headed for the center of town. No one interrupted the soldiers as they entered the newly constructed customs house and ascended the stairs to the roof. As the citizens looked on, the Stars and Stripes, a flag that had not flown above the city for more than eighteen months, unfurled in the wind. Thirty minutes later, the flag came down, and the Federal landing party returned to its boat and rowed back to their ship, completing the symbolic capture of the port.

Having taken the town, Commodore Renshaw faced a serious problem. Admiral Farragut had ordered him to tighten the blockade along the Texas coast; the Commodore had done exactly that, taking Galveston without a casualty. But now he had to hold his gains. The two-mile railroad bridge connecting the island to the mainland—crossing water too shallow to be patrolled by his ships—would have to be left standing, Renshaw reasoned, or the population of the city would starve. His fleet could control the town, he believed, but at least a few hundred infantrymen would be required for patrol and guard duty.

Renshaw dispatched a celebratory message to Farragut in New Orleans, outlining his achievement and position while including the inevitable request for troops. He also remarked on the pro-Union sentiment he found in the city and the rumors of dissension among the population in the interior.

Renshaw left Galveston later that month to raid farther along the coast. With his two shallowest draft vessels, the *Westfield* and *Clifton*, he moved to capture Port Lavaca. After entering the bay, the ships captured the schooner *Lecompte* without a fight and took it in tow. At 1 P.M. on October 31, Renshaw informed the Texan garrison commander of Port Lavaca, Major Daniel D. Shea, of his intentions, allowing ninety minutes for civilians to be removed from the town. Afterward the Federals commenced dueling with two Confederate batteries. In the opening rounds, the *Westfield* burst its heaviest gun, and thereafter the fight was inconclusive. Renshaw ordered his ships out of range for the night. The next day, he resumed the battle from long range, but retreated when he found the Texan gunners still game for the contest. In all his ships had fired 252 shots at the Texans—mostly from 32-pounders and eight-inch Columbiads—without killing a man. The town, though, was a wreck. "The enemy succeeded in doing considerable damage to the town," Shea reported, "tearing up the streets and riddling the houses and otherwise damaging the place."

Even so, Renshaw became uneasy as the Texas coast proved increasingly difficult to subdue. Union sailors went ashore at Point Bolivar to forage for fresh provisions, only to be ambushed and shotgunned by Confederate cavalrymen. Elsewhere, Texans captured a small launch and crew that had also gone ashore. Renshaw felt confident that Galveston was indefensible for the Rebels and wrote Farragut requesting that the town be abandoned until infantry could be landed. The admiral refused, however, proudly announcing that ground troops were already on their way.

Other signs contributed to Renshaw's uneasiness. Off Sabine Pass, the crew of the *Rachel Seaman* was agitated and fearful of Rebel designs. They reported that the Texans had marshaled six steamers of various sizes and several schooners. These ships, armed with heavy guns brought in from Louisiana, would almost certainly make a foray against the *Rachel Seaman*, and its crew feared for their safety. For the commodore, this was indeed unsettling news.

Plagued as he was by these growing threats, Renshaw must have believed that the land itself lay against him. In his various scouting expeditions, he manifested a knack for getting his flagship, the *Westfield*, lodged on the shallow Texas sandbars. In his raid to Port Lavaca, for instance, his ship had grounded a half-dozen times. After each episode, the crew of the *Clifton* diligently brought their ship alongside and dragged their commodore free. The *Clifton*, one officer quipped, was little more than Renshaw's personal tugboat. Superstitious of his sour

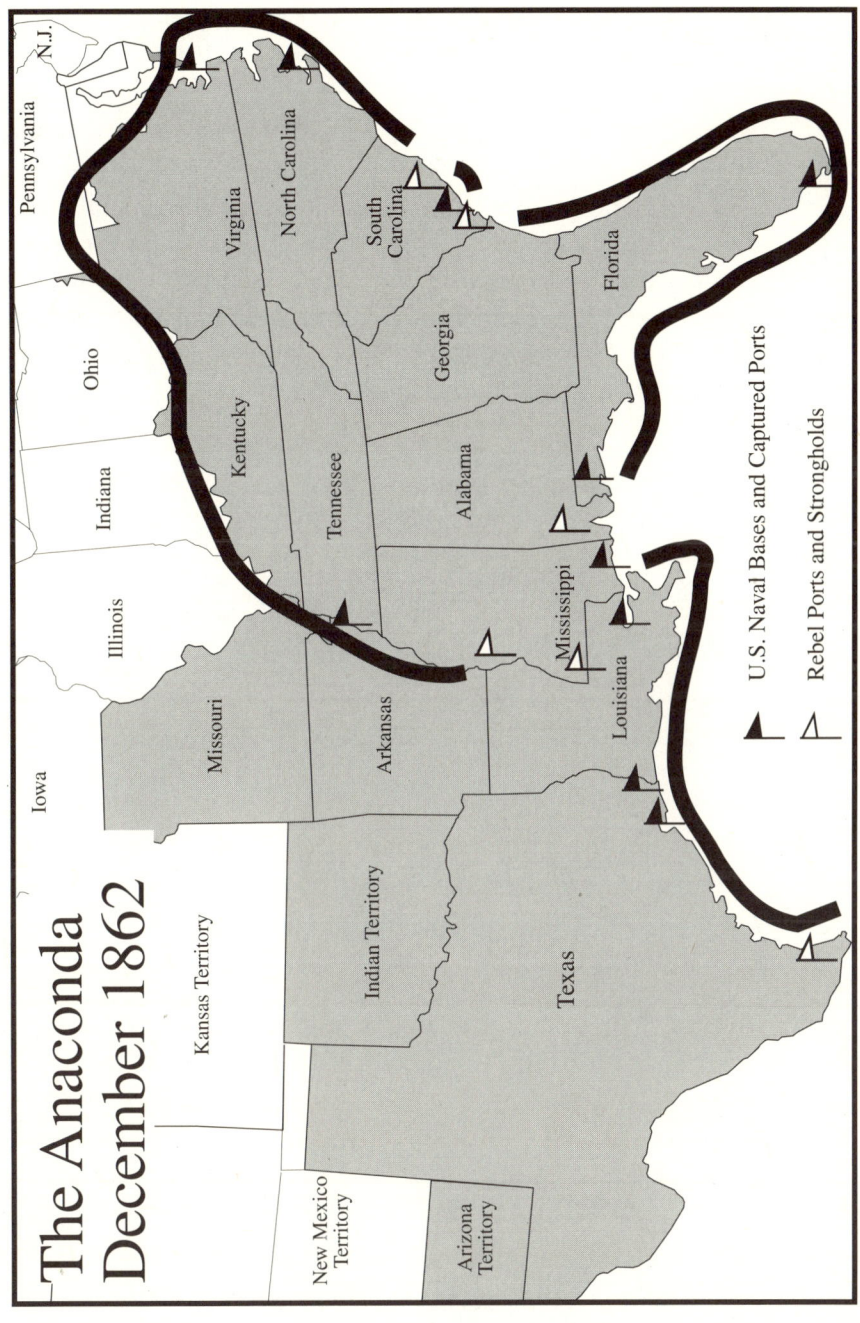

The Anaconda
December 1862

U.S. Naval Bases and Captured Ports

Rebel Ports and Strongholds

luck, the commodore decided to curb further explorations and stay in Galveston until the army could arrive.

By November 1862, the initial phase of Farragut's plan had worked. Union warships made frequent captures off the coast of Louisiana and Texas. Sabine Pass, although never occupied, lay blocked. Galveston would soon feel the tramp of Union infantry. From Calcasieu to Corpus Christi, the U.S. Navy felt victorious. Nothing, so it seemed in the last months of 1862, could defeat the ships of the West Gulf Blockading Squadron. Even so, Farragut and his subordinates tried to leave little to chance, and prepared to maintain, and expand, their conquests.

3
UNIONISTS, GUNBOATS, AND PLASTER BARRELS

For the Federal war effort, the prospect of a Unionist enclave on the Texas coast was extremely exciting. Secretary of War Edwin M. Stanton hoped to reconstitute state governments in any of the Confederate states where a toehold could be made. Usually, the plan was for Unionists in the state concerned to aid the Northern plan by providing a cadre of loyalists with which to legitimize and implement the actions of the installed politicians. Galveston would serve as the Federal capital of the State of Texas.

The U.S. 1st Texas Cavalry would provide the legitimizing military presence. Composed of a wide variety of Texans, including a large proportion of immigrant Germans and Hispanics, this unit had been dubbed the "1st Texas Traitors" by Confederates. Its leadership included many veteran Lone

Star politicians who, for various reasons, had chosen to back the Union upon the advent of secession. The thousand-man regiment would sail to Galveston without horses, but with saddles adequate for mounting it and another regiment. The hope of Union planners was that horses and recruits would be obtained from the state's disaffected citizenry. Ultimately, this cell of Unionist soldiers would become the nucleus of an army to invade the interior with the ultimate goal of capturing Houston and securing the rail line between Hempstead and Beaumont.

While Federal planners and politicians contemplated this master stroke, Renshaw prepared to defend Galveston against what he considered the inevitable counterattack. Confederate cavalry patrols that frequently visited the city via the intact railroad bridge aggravated his suspicions. At Virginia Point hundreds of men drilled in sight of the Union ships. But the Yankees were prepared: in the channel four powerful gunboats lay at anchor, their heavy guns pointing toward the city and their netting raised to repel boarders.

In late December Renshaw had received a portion of his desired infantry, a minor miracle. Whaleboats from the transport *Saxon* landed a 240-man detachment, companies D, G, and I of the 42nd Massachusetts Infantry Regiment, on Kuhn's Wharf at the end of Eighteenth Street. These men lacked experience, having recently arrived at New Orleans from Readville, Massachusetts, where the regiment had been raised. Their greatcoats, the product of an ambitious New England contractor, were black instead of the regular sky blue, and the dye seeped freely with every rain while the cloth itself disintegrated. Shoddily dressed as they were, the Massachusetts's men were at least infantry, and their model 1842 Springfield Muskets and model 1861 Springfield Rifles were oddly reassuring to the crews of the big-bore naval guns. Along with these troops, a replacement cannon for the *Westfield* arrived. The remaining seven companies of the 42nd Massachusetts, Edmund J.

Davis's cavalry, and a battery of Vermont artillery were still in transit.

Colonel Isaac Burrell traveled by ship's boat to report to Renshaw. Upon arriving aboard the *Westfield,* the colonel discovered the admiral entertaining Confederate officers, so the introductory interview had to be deferred. When Burrell finally

Isaac S. Burrell: born Massachusetts 1821; appointed colonel of the 42d Massachusetts Volunteer Militia in August 1862; described by a contemporary as "a tall, middle-aged, wiry-looking soldier," Burrell was captured during the Battle of Galveston in 1863 and detained in a Houston, Texas, warehouse, where he and other Federal officers were allowed to roam the city after promising "not to attempt to escape or pass beyond the limits of Houston until exchanged"; later held prisoner at both Camp Groce, near Hempstead, and Camp Ford, near Tyler, Texas; a fellow prisoner recalled Burrell once saying "he was so cold that he feared he was dying"; he was paroled at Red River Lodge, Louisiana, in July 1864. "About a thousand Union prisoners, mostly taken over a year, and some nearly two years ago, arrived in this city on Sunday, having been exchanged," reported the *New Orleans Daily Picayune* on July 26, 1864. "Among them were some officers and seamen of the navy. Col. Burrell, of the 42d Massachusetts, a nine months' regiment, has been a prisoner since January 1st, 1863, double the time of the entire term of his regiment." Burrell was mustered out of service at Boston in August 1864. Years after the Civil War, he was appointed "marshal of the day" at a Washington's birthday celebration, during which Burrell "acknowledged the honor conferred upon him, but thought one of fewer years than himself, whose sands of life were now nearly run out, might better

have been chosen from among so many gentlemen of legal and literary attainments present, of which he possessed none"; at another time in a gubernatorial election "the most enthusiastic and indefatigable" brought Burrell to cast his ballot "in his rocking-chair"; he voted "the straight Union ticket."

did get an audience, he petitioned for his troops to be quartered on Pelican Spit instead of Kuhn's Wharf until reinforcements arrived. Renshaw listened patiently, then, with assurances that the navy would see to the soldiers' protection, ordered the infantry to remain in the city where water supplies were more plentiful. Anxious over the safety of his command, Burrell ceased his protests only after repeated assurances that the gunboats would never abandon the 42nd Massachusetts. In fact, Renshaw argued, the entire detachment could be evacuated by boat in five minutes should any situation became dangerous. Burrell, his fears somewhat allayed, saluted smartly and returned to his command.

The wobbly-legged infantry, glad to be back on shore, prepared their position well. Colonel Burrell quartered his men in a two-story warehouse on Kuhn's Wharf; while their accommodations were cramped, the position was immediately under the guns of the fleet as promised. As further protection, Burrell ordered the planks closest to shore taken up and stacked to build a stout barricade across the width of the wharf. In addition to providing a breastwork, this action left a protective gap of water between themselves and any enemy approach. Soldiers constructed a second line made of bricks, barrels of dry plaster, and lumber taken from inside the adjacent warehouse. An opening remained in both walls to allow access to pickets, but huge sacks of cottonseed remained nearby to close them in event of an attack. A single board remained to join the wharf to the shore.

Company ordnance officers, however, carried bad news. In the hurry to get the troops to Galveston, improper cargo handling had landed Burrell's command with a shortage of ammunition. Companies D and I, with smoothbore muskets, had a shortage of "buck and ball" cartridges appropriate to their weapons. Company G, armed with rifles, had an over-abundance of cartridges; all suffered from a shortage of percussion caps. The ammunition mix-up left each soldier with only eighteen shots in his cartridge box.

This bad news rekindled Colonel Burrell's fears, prompting that officer to launch a reconnaissance to determine the extent of the enemy threat. On the morning of December 26, Commander Wainwright of the *Harriet Lane* and a party of sailors, pistols and cutlasses in hand, arrived on Kuhn's Wharf and, together with 100 men of the 42nd Massachusetts, traveled through town looking for Rebel scouts. After discovering most of the inhabitants to either be gone, or non-communicative, the expedition proceeded two miles past the city toward Eagle Grove. Fearful of any further advance, the party returned to the wharf after establishing a lookout post in a cupola atop a four story brick building on The Strand.

This exploration, coupled by an afternoon scout by the *Harriet Lane* toward the railroad bridge, convinced Burrell that danger was indeed close at hand. Texans manned a three-gun earthwork at Eagle Grove and a large fortification at Virginia Point, thus securing both ends of the bridge. The structure's mid-point—the draw span—lay guarded by another heavy gun. At the same time, water depth did not permit a single heavy warship then in the harbor to proceed close enough to either position to menace the Rebels with their cannon or hit the bridge with any degree of accuracy. Burrell, now given almost completely over to anxiety, knew that as long as that avenue of approach lay open to the Confederates, the Bay State men on Kuhn's Wharf would sleep few peaceful nights.

Later that week Burrell expressed his concerns in a dispatch to his superior, General Nathaniel P. Banks, back in New Orleans. "During the day, we control the city," he wrote. He was also mindful that after dark, sentries reported Texas horsemen moving among the shadows. "But at night, owing to our small force...I am obliged to draw in the pickets to the wharf on which we are quartered."

The men with the muskets, though, had a potent fleet at their backs, and Renshaw positioned his ships to what he considered their best advantage. The picturesque and heavily armed U.S.S. *Harriet Lane*, anchored in the middle of the channel off Twenty-Ninth Street, was farthest west in the naval battleline. Named for James Buchanan's niece and originally commissioned as a revenue cutter in 1852, the ship was already a seasoned veteran. The *Harriet Lane* had fired the first shots of the war by the U.S. Navy on April 12, 1861, in defense of Fort Sumter. The ship had also helped pummel forts Jackson and St. Philip below New Orleans. Aboard were 130 veteran sailors and marines, serving six guns. A fast, well-built ship carrying

U.S.S. *Harriet Lane*

two IX-inch Dahlgrens and two 32-pound smoothbores in each broadside, a IX-inch Dahlgren pivot gun forward of her paddle wheels, and a 20-pounder Parrot rifle pivot gun in the bow, most of its crew considered the *Harriet Lane* the darling of the Galveston Squadron.

One other veteran ship rocked at anchor in the channel just off the line of docks and wharves. The side-wheel steamer U.S.S. *Clifton* had originally been a New York harbor ferryboat; she became Navy property late in 1861 and added her arsenal of six cannon—four 32-pounders and two IX-inch Dahlgren

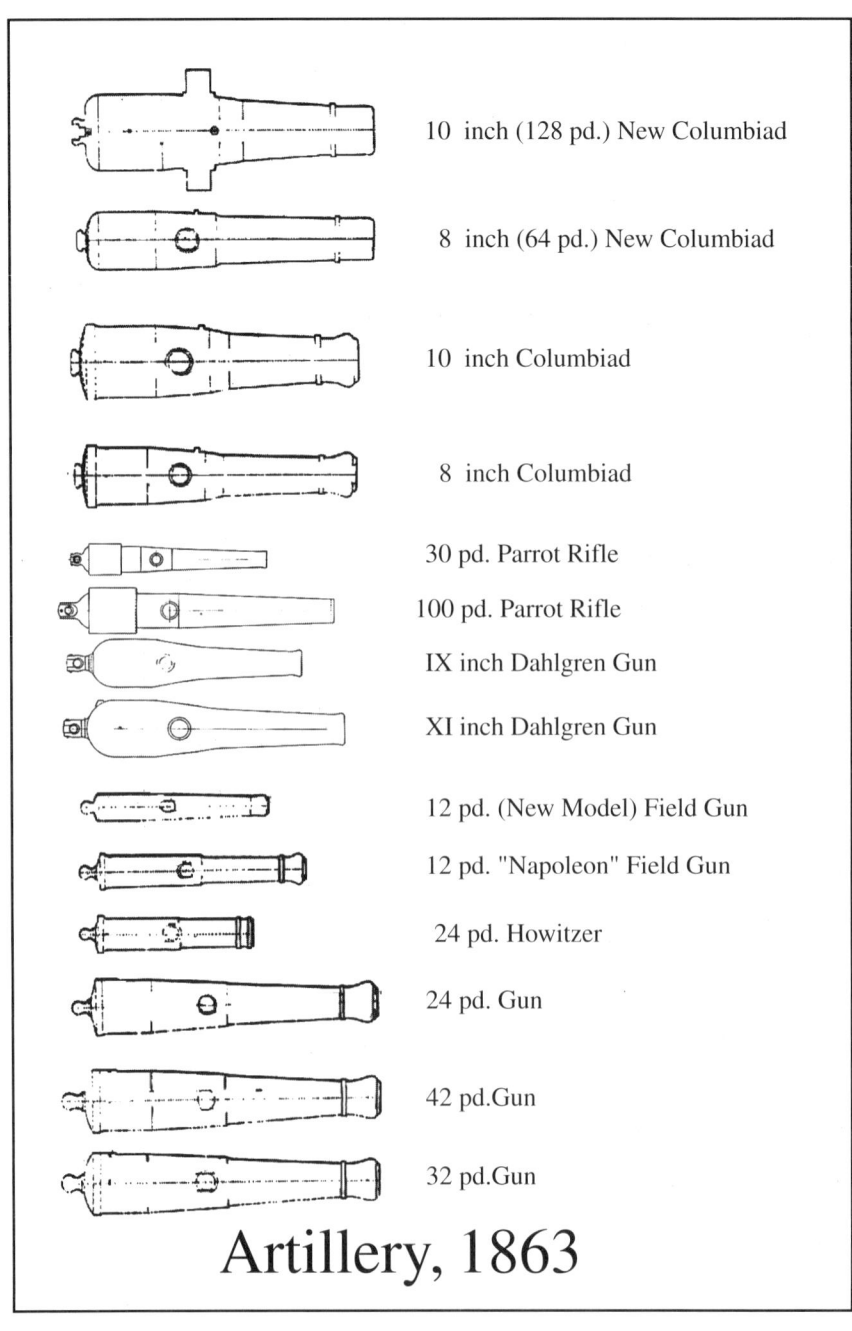

10 inch (128 pd.) New Columbiad

8 inch (64 pd.) New Columbiad

10 inch Columbiad

8 inch Columbiad

30 pd. Parrot Rifle

100 pd. Parrot Rifle

IX inch Dahlgren Gun

XI inch Dahlgren Gun

12 pd. (New Model) Field Gun

12 pd. "Napoleon" Field Gun

24 pd. Howitzer

24 pd. Gun

42 pd. Gun

32 pd. Gun

Artillery, 1863

smoothbores—to the weight of the fleet. This vessel, like most of the others in the bay, had fought its way up the Mississippi, receiving damage from Rebel guns at Vicksburg before returning to the Gulf.

The other two Federal warships lay anchored a mile away near Pelican Spit, protecting the troop transports from any Confederate vessels that might appear. Like the *Clifton*, the side wheel gunboat U.S.S. *Westfield* had once been a New York ferryboat. After being purchased by the navy, this ship sailed the Mississippi until Commodore Renshaw made it the flagship of his Galveston Squadron. Powerfully armed, the *Westfield* carried four eight-inch new model Columbiad smoothbores in broadside, one IX inch Dahlgren in stern pivot, and, until recently, one 100-pounder Parrot rifle in a bow pivot.

The U.S.S. *Owasco*, a "90 Day Gunboat" designed specifically for blockade service, carried a 20-pounder Parrot pivot gun in the bow, an XI-inch Dahlgren in pivot amidships, and a 24-pounder howitzer on either broadside. It, like the *Westfield*, *Clifton*, and *Harriet Lane*, had seen action below New Orleans.

On December 29, the fleet received reinforcements in the form of the propeller-driven U.S.S. *Sachem* escorted by the U.S.S. *Corypheus*. Having served along the Texas coast since August, *Sachem* was the oldest of the U.S. vessels on station and was a frequent visitor to Mustang Island, having recently engaged in a heated duel with Confederates at Aransas Pass. It had steamed into Galveston Bay seeking repairs to its boiler. A crew of fifty served the ship's two 32-pounders in each broadside and a 20-pound Parrot rifle in the bow.

The *Sachem's* escort, the schooner *Corypheus*, also lay near Kuhn's Wharf. The smallest of the Federal warships in Galveston Bay, it had been a Confederate blockade runner until its capture in Bayou Bonfuca, Louisiana, in May 1862. Now the sailing vessel flew U.S. colors, and its crew of twenty-eight manned two pivoting guns—a 24-pounder howitzer in the stern and a 30-pounder Parrot rifle in the bow.

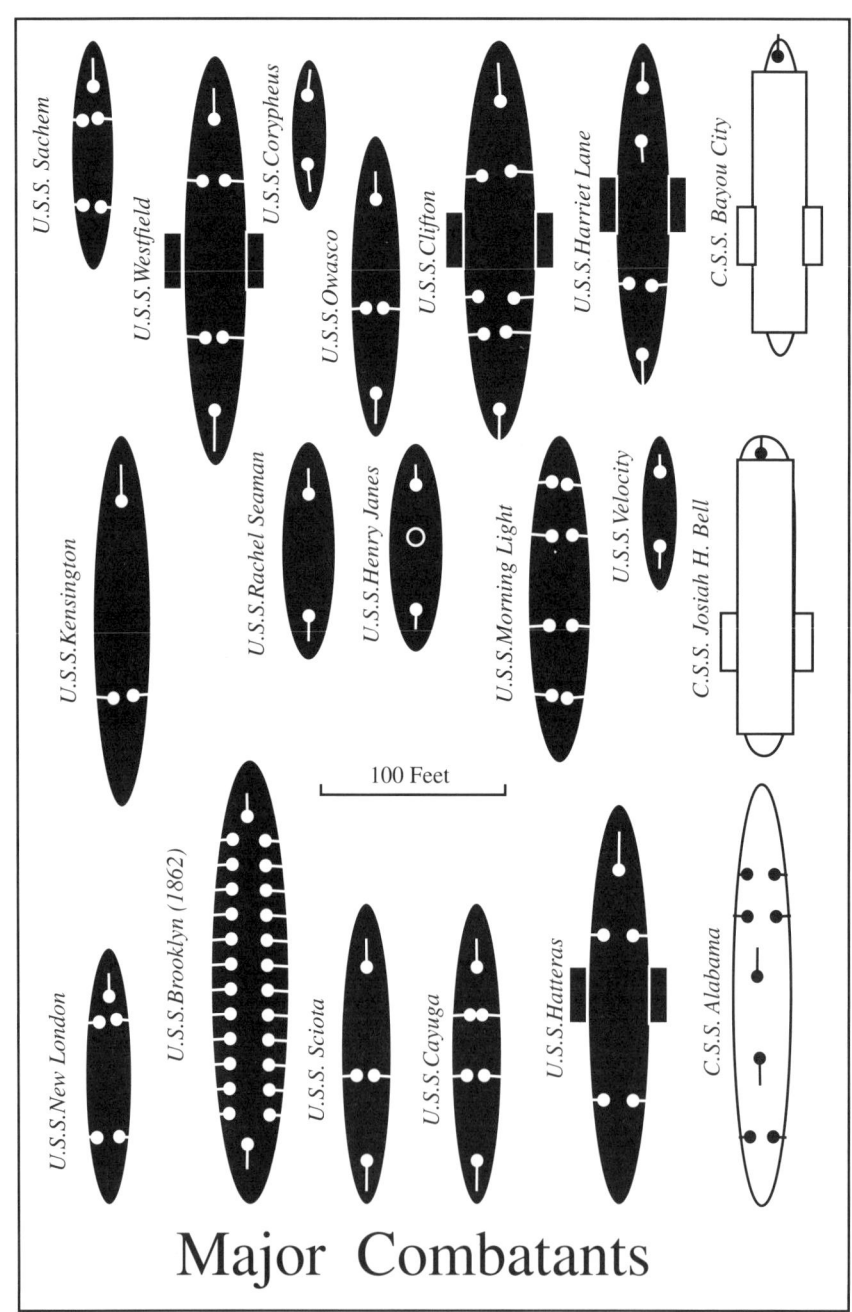

U.S.S. Sachem
U.S.S.Westfield
U.S.S.Corypheus
U.S.S.Owasco
U.S.S.Clifton
U.S.S.Harriet Lane
C.S.S. Bayou City

U.S.S.Kensington
U.S.S.Rachel Seaman
U.S.S.Henry Janes
U.S.S.Morning Light
U.S.S.Velocity
C.S.S. Josiah H. Bell

U.S.S.New London
U.S.S.Brooklyn (1862)
U.S.S. Sciota
U.S.S.Cayuga
U.S.S.Hatteras
C.S.S. Alabama

100 Feet

Major Combatants

Renshaw felt secure even if Burrell did not. Days later when the storm-battered *Mary A. Boardman* arrived bearing the 2nd Vermont Battery, couriers delivered news informing the commodore that besides the balance of the 42nd Massachusetts, he would soon be managing the landing of more than a thousand additional Federal soldiers—the men and saddles of the Union 1st Texas Cavalry. This combined brigade would be commanded by Edmund J. Davis, the arch-Unionist of Texas. Confident in his ability to hold the town until the rest of that column arrived, Renshaw spent a peaceful holiday season on the Texas coast, looking forward to what the New Year, and the Confederate States, might offer.

4
PRINCE JOHN'S NAVY

Confederate Texans found little to celebrate during the Christmas season of 1862. The military situation in the state was a shambles. With little opposition, enemy troops had occupied most of the strategic points along the Texas Gulf coast. Friends and family lay dead on the distant battlefields of Virginia, Tennessee, and Arkansas. And finally, the ignoble venture into New Mexico, launched amid high expectations the previous year, had failed dismally, adding more names to the casualty list. As a result of these reverses, a feeling of pessimism gripped the population.

In November 1862, the Richmond government sent a new commander to Texas who elicited both optimism and suspicion—Major General John B. Magruder. Nicknamed "Prince John" because of his courtly manner, Magruder had won three brevet promotions for gallantry during the Mexican War. In 1861 he had successfully commanded Confederate forces in the Peninsular Campaign of Virginia. But Prince John also had his failings. In June 1862, General Robert E. Lee, commander of the Army of Northern Virginia, charged Magruder with several mistakes in the Seven Days Battle around Richmond and

John Bankhead Magruder: born Virginia 1807; Magruder was graduated from the U.S. Military Academy in 1830, fifteenth in his class of forty-two; commissioned 2d lieutenant and posted to infantry, he soon transferred to the 1st Artillery; promoted to 1st lieutenant in 1836, he served in the Seminole Wars and in Texas; he distinguished himself in the Mexican War, earning brevets for Palo Alto, Cerro Gordo, and Chapultepec; he was promoted to captain in 1846, served on the frontier, and commanded the post at Newport, Rhode Island; with the secession of Virginia, he resigned his commission to enter Confederate service; commissioned a colonel, he rose quickly through the ranks, gaining promotion to brigadier general in June 1861 and major general in October; placed in command of Rebel troops on the Virginia Peninsula, Magruder fought and won the first battle in that state at Big Bethel in June 1861; due to his flamboyant manner and dress he earned the sobriquet "Prince John"; in the spring of 1862 he masterfully deceived the Federals during the early stages of the Peninsular Campaign by creating the impression that his force was much larger than it actually was; but during the Seven Days' Battles Magruder buckled under the strain, prompting accusations of drunkenness; sent to the Trans-Mississippi shortly thereafter, he took command of the District of Texas, New Mexico, and Arizona—a position he held until the end of the war and discharged with great energy; in January 1863 he directed the recapture of Galveston and, in the spring of 1864, dispatched the bulk of his command to assist General Richard

Taylor in Louisiana during the Red River Expedition; throughout Magruder's tenure Texas remained relatively untouched by the Federals; refusing to surrender at the close of the Civil War, he fled to Mexico, where he became a general in the service of Emperor Maximilian; upon the fall of Maximilian in 1867, he returned to the United States, making a living as a lecturer; General Magruder died at Houston, Texas, in 1871; he remains among the war's most colorful characters.

accepted his resignation from command. Prince John had furthermore earned a reputation as a heavy drinker; many speculated that his taste for whiskey had landed him in this remote department, far from the glory in the east. Despite the rumors, Magruder won support by bringing to Texas a scheme for reversing the state's recent military disasters. He hoped to regain the harbors of the upper Texas coast. Most importantly, for reasons both military and symbolic, he planned to recover the city of Galveston.

The key, he realized upon taking stock of his new command, was gunboats. He took inventory of the floating stock at Sabine Lake and Galveston Bay, and found a number of likely candidates. Mostly small river steamers or packet boats, they were poor platforms for the weight of heavy weapons and armor.

Weapons and armor, though, were what he earnestly desired. Magruder, having witnessed close-hand the effect of the ironclad, cannon-armed C.S.S. *Virginia* on wooden vessels off Hampton Roads, Virginia, in March 1862, wanted to build an ironclad of his own. Having surveyed the shipbuilding facilities on Buffalo Bayou in Houston, he soon realized that Texas—indeed the whole of the Trans-Mississippi—would be sorely pressed to achieve such an ambitious goal. Even if the iron could be scrounged, the weapons could not.

Texas was long on one commodity. Cotton, pressed into 500-pound bales, would have to serve as armor. Field pieces or obsolete naval guns would have to suffice for the gunboats' offensive punch. Magruder ordered the construction of as many of these "cottonclads" as the yards at Houston and Beaumont could turn out, with a hoped-for delivery date of Christmas Day.

At Houston, the Confederate government had purchased several steamboats capable of carrying sizable boarding parties: the *Bayou City*, a river steamer serving as a police boat in Galveston Bay; the *Neptune*, a former mail packet; and two smaller vessels, the *John F. Carr* and *Lucy Gwinn*. At Harrisburg, workers assembled cotton bales, lumber, and cannon to convert the newly acquired vessels into Prince John's fleet. The commodore of this fleet would be Major Leon Smith of the Confederate Army, a steamboat skipper Magruder had known in California. Prince John awarded Smith the naval rank of captain, and made him commodore in charge of his Texas flotilla.

By the end of the year, the Confederate fleet had undergone an amazing transformation in Harrisburg. Workers removed the upper cabin, or "Texas," and pilot house from the C.S.S.

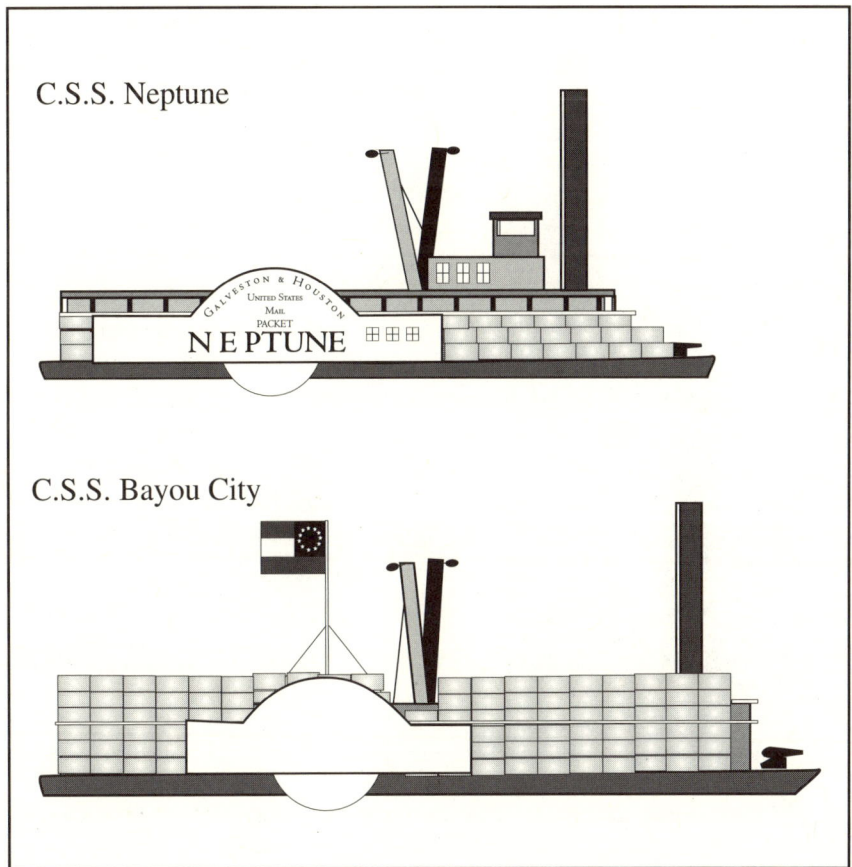

C.S.S. Neptune

GALVESTON & HOUSTON
UNITED STATES
MAIL
PACKET
NEPTUNE

C.S.S. Bayou City

Bayou City. Cotton bales placed on their narrow sides three high, backed by another row lying flat, provided breastworks and firing platforms for sharpshooters. Remodeling had given the wooden steamer the rakish look of an ironclad ram, if not the potency. Two boarding planks, designed to drop onto enemy vessels' decks like a Roman *corvus*, had been constructed to the rear of the *Bayou City's* smokestacks. The bow of the gunboat sported a refurbished 32-pounder, converted into a rifle. Captain Henry S. Lubbock, brother of the state's governor, would command this, the flagship of the flotilla.

The rest of the fleet also neared completion. C.S.S. *Neptune*, under the direction of Captain William S. Sangster, also emerged as a cottonclad, its rectangular white "armor" stacked much like a cotton transport of ante-bellum days. The *Neptune* carried two 24-pounder field howitzers as its armament. Cotton protected the boiler of the cannonless C.S.S.

Courtesy of the Rosenberg Library, Galveston, Texas

Leon Smith: born "near the ocean" in either Maine or Connecticut, he went to sea at the age of thirteen; by the time he was twenty, Smith commanded the mail steamship *Pacific*, which sailed between San Francisco and Panama; while engaged in shipping on the West Coast in the late 1840s, Smith met John B. Magruder, with whom he would later be associated in warfare along the Texas Coast; during the 1850s, Smith shifted his sailing activities to the Gulf of Mexico and became associated with the Southern Mail Steamship Company owned by Charles Morgan, whose ships had been sailing between New Orleans and Galveston since 1835; when Smith became associated with him, Morgan's firm was large enough for a government official to claim it did "all the business in the Gulf." After Texas left the Union in 1861, arrangements were made to send John S. Ford to Brownsville to receive the surrender of the U.S. forces there; Smith, as captain of the *General Rusk*, transported Ford and his troops, sailing from Galveston on February 19, 1861; two

John F. Carr; C.S.S. *Lucy Gwinn*, which served as a wood tender for the squadron, was defenseless. Captain John Wier of Company B, 1st Texas Heavy Artillery, volunteered himself and his men to serve aboard the *Bayou City* as gunners; Company C manned the guns of the *Neptune*.

In Sabine Lake, the Confederacy's newest men-of-war were the *Uncle Ben* and the *Josiah H. Bell*. They, however, would not be ready until after the first of the year.

Magruder planned to free the Texas coast in two phases. First, he wanted to recover Galveston. This seemed to be the easiest of his tasks since the Federals lay close to shore and could be attacked by land forces. The Confederate attack would be a fairly complicated attempt to coordinate land and naval forces, but Magruder believed it could be done. Second, he planned a naval sortie from Sabine Lake to capture the blockading vessels off Sabine Pass.

days later they arrived at Brownsville, and Ford received the surrender of the Federal troops; Ford's official report expressed his "many obligations to Captain Leon Smith of the steamer *General Rusk* for efficient service promptly rendered during the voyage"; after removing the Federal troops from Brownsville to New York, Smith was back by mid-April in familiar Gulf waters preparing to back the Confederate cause; the steamer *General Rusk* and her crew became "volunteers" in the Confederate Navy. His most daring exploits came in 1863 when he commanded the Confederate flotilla at the Battle of Galveston on January 1, and when he fought at Sabine Pass in September; though Smith never held a regular commission from the Confederate Government, General John B. Magruder, commander of the District of Texas, Arizona, and New Mexico, had particular faith in the sailor's ability and eventually conferred upon him the *de facto* command of all ships serving the Texas Marine Department; in 1864 Magruder dispatched Smith to England with plans for purchasing a commerce raider paid for with proceeds from cotton smuggled from Galveston and Sabine Pass; Smith made it as far as Havana when the war ended. After the war, Smith was reunited with his wife and son at San Francisco before drifting to Fort Wrangel in the recently acquired Alaska Territory; here he served as a merchant and billiard hall proprietor; during a personal altercation, Smith died at the hands of a Stickine Indian on the day after Christmas 1869; he was buried in San Franciso.

Magruder ordered area infantry, cavalry, and artillery units to make themselves ready for the upcoming expedition. He ordered the untried 20th Texas Infantry and the inexperienced 21st Texas Infantry Battalion into camps at Virginia Point. Detachments of the 26th Texas Cavalry, led by the flamboyant French mercenary Colonel Xavier Debray, patrolled Galveston Island. The veterans of the 2d Texas Cavalry, who called themselves with some justification the "oldest regiment in Confederate service," also moved to Virginia Point. Three

Xavier Blanchard Debray: born France 1819; graduated from the French Military Academy before migrating to the United States in 1848; received his citizenship in 1855, at San Antonio, Texas, where he published a Spanish-language newspaper, and worked as a translator in the General Land Office at Austin; with the secession

of Texas, he joined the Tom Green Rifles as a 1st lieutenant, but was soon appointed aide-de-camp to Governor Francis R. Lubbock; eventually elected colonel 26th Texas Cavalry; during 1862, Debray commanded a sub-district in Texas that included Galveston, and was conspicuously engaged in the re-capture of that city in January 1863; his commander Major General John B. Magruder commended him for his "coolness and courage" as well as his leadership; in April 1864 Major General Richard Taylor wrote that "the soldierly qualities displayed by the Colonel, and the good conduct of his men, meet the acknowledgment of the Major-General commanding, who has every reason to form brilliant expectations of the future career of this fine corps." Debray and his regiment earned more praise at Mansfield and Pleasant Hill; although Debray was promoted to brigadier general by order of General E. Kirby Smith, in April 1864, President Jefferson Davis never made that appointment official; commanded a brigade of Texas cavalry until discharged, in March 1865; Debray eventually returned to his job at the General Land Office, and died at Austin 1895. A gifted cavalry officer, Debray spent the entire war in the obscurity of the Trans-Mississippi.

artillery batteries, bringing with them fifteen rifled and smoothbore field pieces, rumbled into camp as well. Those gunners of Colonel Joseph J. Cook's 1st Texas Heavy Artillery who were not already employed crewing field pieces or serving aboard the gunboats collected and served a half-dozen heavier cannon. These included the largest gun on the Texas coast, the eight-inch Columbiad mounted on a "railway ram"—a flatcar covered with iron rails and cross-ties to form a casemated, but mobile, emplacement. This collection of mostly raw Confederates exhausted the available manpower on the upper coast—with the exception, that is, of Henry Hopkins Sibley's shot-up brigade of exhausted New Mexico Campaign veterans who lay in camps some fifty miles away.

5

"Rangers of the Prairie, Rangers of the Sea"

The New Mexico disaster, launched in the fall of 1861 in an effort to extend the Confederacy to the Pacific, had nearly ruined both Confederate Brigadier General Henry Hopkins Sibley and his brigade. After marching across western Texas and into New Mexico in the height of winter, Sibley's Brigade had fought two major battles, Val Verde in February and Glorieta in March, and several skirmishes before abandoning the expedition in the late spring of 1862. By July 1862, after bringing his disorganized and demoralized command back to San Antonio, Sibley found his reputation in jeopardy over misconduct of the campaign. He faced serious charges—cowardice and drunkenness. Confederate Adjutant General Samuel Cooper ordered him to Richmond, Virginia, for an explanation. While he tended to this matter, Sibley placed his senior

James Reily: born Ohio; moved to Kentucky as a youth and studied law in the office of Judge Robert Todd; after being admitted to the bar, Reily married Ellen Hart, the niece of Henry Clay; the couple moved to Texas and settled in Nacogdoches in 1836 or 1837; they soon moved to Houston, where Reily first gained public attention as the captain of the Milam Guards in a campaign against Indians; he served as a major in the army of the Texas Republic, and later gained recognition in the field of diplomacy; nominated district attorney for the Fifth Judical District, but the Texas Senate refused to confirm Reily's nomination; after

serving as Harris County's representative in the Fifth Congress of the Republic of Texas, he was twice, in 1841 and again in 1844, appointed by President Sam Houston minister to the United States, but Reily's opposition to annexation prevented his nomination from being confirmed; he commanded a Texas regiment during the Mexican War; an influential Whig, he bolted the party in 1855 because of its anti-slavery agitation and backed James Buchanan for president; named consul to Russia in payment, Reily soon resigned; back in Houston by 1861, he used his oratorical skills in support of secession; commissioned colonel of the 4th Texas Mounted Volunteers, Reily became a key diplomat in General H. H. Sibley's New Mexico Campaign. "We must have Sonora and Chihuahua," Reily announced. "With Sonora and Chihuahua we gain Southern California, and by a railroad to Guaymas render...Texas the great highway of nations." With Sibley's approval, he left his regiment to engage in diplomatic relations with Mexican officials but failed to gain any firm commitments; he was in fact no more successful diplomatically than Sibley and his Texans were militarily; the New Mexico Campaign was almost over before Reily rejoined his regiment; he later served during the Battle of Galveston and thereafter in Louisiana, where he was killed at the Battle of Irish Bend in 1863 "leading his men into the battle." A pious man, Reily served for many years as vestryman in the Episcopal church; when in the field he regularly held preaching services.

colonel, James Reily of the 4th Texas Cavalry, in temporary command of the brigade, which Reily, in turn, furloughed to their homes. The men had departed for sixty days; because of a lack of supplies, officers extended the furlough and as a result, troops remained scattered across the state until recalled at the end of the year.

Tom Green, one of Sibley's colonels and arguably one of the most popular men in Texas before the war, had also become a casualty of the New Mexico Campaign—wounded not in body but in reputation. As the Confederacy's great drive for empire had come unwound on the upper Rio Grande, disgruntled soldiers placed much of the blame on Tom Green—the hero of Val Verde. They claimed that he had been drunk during much of the expedition. As a result, the man who had won the largest fight of the offensive found himself passed over for promotion. William Read Scurry, a lieutenant colonel in the brigade, and William Steele, a junior colonel, both received advancement to brigadier general. Tom Green instead fought to salvage his reputation.

December 1862 was also a trying month for the rank and file veterans of Sibley's Brigade. The weather was miserable, shelter scarce. The designation of several brigade mustering points created confusion; many soldiers could not find their commands as they wandered from town to town searching for their brigade headquarters. Eventually, a majority of the men made their way to Cypress City, the 4th Texas Cavalry rendezvous, and to Hempstead, bivouac of the 5th and 7th regiments. Upon arriving at camp, the troops discovered a critical lack of supplies as well as many new members of the brigade—volunteers and conscripts—who had yet to be trained. After several months at home, even the most ardent warriors were reluctant to return to duty.

Once back in camp, the troops suspected a fight was imminent. Immediately upon reaching their bivouacs, the men were ordered on a tiring sixty-mile ride to Houston, where they expected to face the enemy. Once there, however, they were ordered to reverse the journey and return to their camps. Instructions called for the dismounting of the regiments with the men to remain near the Galveston, Houston, and Henderson Railroad. A detail grazed the brigade mounts in nearby pastures while the cavalrymen practiced infantry movements. The senseless orders, extra drill, and tighter discipline all pointed to an impending battle.

For Sibley's Brigade, the Galveston campaign began to unfold in the dark early morning hours of Christmas Day. The shrill, brassy notes of bugles awakened the tired soldiers at 1:00 A.M. The men then crammed into three trains that waited on the siding to carry them south. By mid-morning, the long trains arrived in Harrisburg, where for the next four days the unit waited. Tiring of the inactivity, Colonel Tom Green of the 5th Texas Cavalry and Colonel Arthur Bagby of the 7th—himself under a cloud for a drinking incident in New Mexico—decided to volunteer their troops as sharpshooters aboard the ships, perhaps as a secret dash of bravado to enhance their reputations. On December 28 the officers departed for Houston to discuss the idea with Magruder and, after some initial hesitation, the general agreed. Green and Bagby quickly returned to Harrisburg to gather their volunteers and inform brigade commander Colonel Reily of the change in orders. The officers reached their camps late in the morning of December 29, but the 4th Texas had already departed by rail for Virginia Point.

The two remaining regiments of the brigade provided the volunteers. Colonel Green ordered the 5th and 7th regiments into line, then addressed the troops: "I want 300 volunteers who are willing to die for Texas, and who are ready to die now. Volunteers will step two paces to the front." The response was so overwhelming that each captain could only choose fifteen men from his company for the duty. The remainder took trains to Virginia Point under the command of Lieutenant Colonel Henry

C. McNeil of the 5th Texas and Major Gustav Hoffman of the 7th.

Joseph Faust, a teen-aged German from New Braunfels, volunteered enthusiastically as did most of his company. "Schwarzhoff, Conrads, and twenty men from our company

Thomas Green: born Virginia 1814; moved with his family to Tennessee in 1817; attended the University of Nashville and Princeton College in Kentucky; practiced law in Tennessee before relocating to Texas in 1835; in the War for Texas Independence, he fought in the Battle of San Jacinto in 1836; served the Republic of Texas as adjutant general of the army, legislator, and soldier in numerous actions against Indians and Mexicans; captain of Texas volunteers with General Zachary Taylor in the Mexican War; clerk of the Texas Supreme Court from 1841 to 1861; at the outbreak of the Civil War he became colonel of the 5th Texas Cavalry; in General Henry Hopkins Sibley's 1862 invasion of New Mexico he commanded

Confederate forces at Val Verde and performed capably throughout the disastrous campaign; in January 1863 he participated in the recapture of Galveston; later that year Sibley's Brigade joined General Richard Taylor's command in Louisiana to oppose General N. P. Banks's Bayou Teche Expedition; when Sibley fell ill, Green assumed direction of the brigade; promoted to brigadier general in May 1863; led the brigade in operations associated with the defense of Vicksburg; in southern Louisiana, he defeated Federal forces at Bayous La Fourche, Fordoche, and Bourbeau after which Taylor recommended Green's promotion to major general; Green's hard-riding troopers were sent back to Texas late in 1863 to oppose a threatened Federal invasion; returned to Louisiana in the spring of 1864 in response to Banks's drive up the Red River; conspicuously engaged at Mansfield and Pleasant Hill; as the Federals retreated, Green, now commanding a cavalry division, was dispatched to harass Union gunboats on the Red River; in an assault on the gunboat *Osage* at Blair's Landing on October 12, Green was killed. General Taylor was lavish in his praise of Green and considered the loss of the Texan "irreparable." General Green indeed owned an impressive record, much of which was won against long odds. His brother-in-law was Confederate General James P. Major.

Arthur P. Bagby: born Alabama 1833, the son of Alabama senator and governor Arthur Pendleton Bagby and his second wife, Anne Connell; graduated from the U.S. Military Academy in 1852, thirty-sixth in his class of forty-three; brevet 2d lieutenant, 8th Infantry, 1852 to 1853; resigned to study law; practiced law in Mobile from 1855 until 1858 when he moved to Gonzales, Texas, where he practiced until appointed major of the 7th Regiment of Texas Mounted Volunteers in 1861; promoted to lieutenant colonel in April 1862 and to full colonel in November 1862; after participating in the unsuccessful invasion of New Mexico and clearing himself on a charge of drunkenness on duty, he led the 7th Texas in the recapture of Galveston in 1863, commanding a detachment of volunteers on a "cottonclad" gunboat; sent to Louisiana as part of General Henry Sibley's (later Thomas Green's) Texas cavalry, Bagby commanded his unit at the Battle of Berwick Bay in April 1863 where he received a wound in the arm but remained on the field until the Federals retreated; upon the promotion of Green to divisional command, Bagby led the Sibley-Green Brigade at the Battles of Fordoche and Bayou Bourbeau; during the Red River Campaign of 1864, Bagby engaged in rear guard actions against the Federal advance; on April 8 at the Battle of Mansfield, his dismounted brigade helped turn the Union right flank; during the Battle of Pleasant Hill on April 9, the brigade, again dismounted, captured an advanced Union position; thereafter, Bagby's calvary harassed the Federal retreat to Simmesport. General E. Kirby Smith, who earlier had recommended Bagby for promotion, assigned the "brilliant" Bagby to duty as brigadier general on April 13, 1864, to date from March 17; later given command of the 4th Brigade, 2d Cavalry Division, Bagby received permanent

command of an entire cavalry division and on May 16, 1865, Kirby Smith promoted him to major general (to rank from May 10), but by then the war had ended. After the peace, Bagby resumed his law career in Victoria, Texas, and from 1870 to 1871 served as assistant editor of the Victoria *Advocate*; in the 1870s he settled in Halletsville, Texas, and established a successful law practice; Bagby, a "learned and a fine orator," continued as an active and prominent lawyer. He died in Halletsville on February 21, 1921, and is buried in the city cemetery.

responded," he wrote home that evening. "The rest of the regiment, too, are to go (to Virginia Point) tomorrow." He realized the gravity of his decision. "Probably we have the most dangerous part. If we succeed, it evidently will be a decision in favor of Texas; if we fail we will either be killed or taken prisoner."

Marching away from their camps at noon on December 31, the Confederate volunteer "horse-marines," armed mostly with Enfield rifles and shotguns, began their new role as they took their places aboard the ships. After reaching the Harrisburg landing, the column divided. The 150 soldiers from the 5th Texas Cavalry moved aboard the *Bayou City*; 100 men from the 7th Texas Cavalry reported to the *Neptune*, and the remaining 50 went aboard the *John F. Carr*. Private Faust of the 7th Texas was not impressed with his battleship. "When we came to the steamboat," he wrote, "we found it a joke."

At the same time, officers completed their battle plans. The

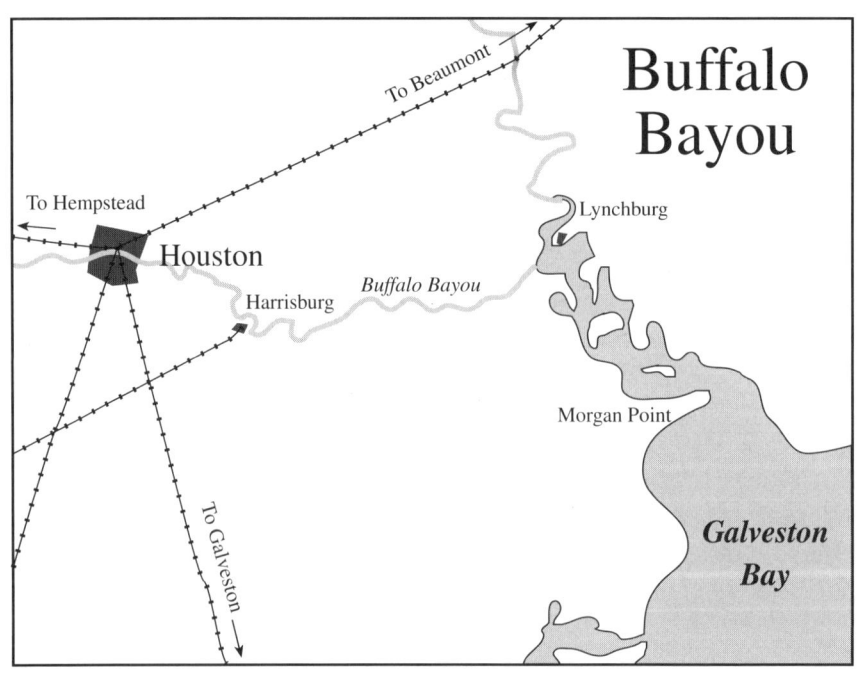

land forces, under the command of Brigadier General Scurry, were to divide, with one portion storming Kuhn's Wharf, another taking positions along The Strand, and Sibley's veterans providing the reserve, assembling around the customs house at the corner of Twentieth and Post Office streets. Artillery, with support from the other assembled regiments, would carry the main attack. The 20th Texas Infantry divided, with most of the companies working to haul the artillery pieces from Eagle Grove to their positions along The Strand. Companies A and B, with troops from the 21st Infantry Battalion and the 2d Texas Cavalry, carried scaling ladders to assault the Federal position at Kuhn's Wharf.

Halfway to Galveston, Confederate engineers had constructed a temporary telegraph station to serve as the final checkpoint between the two elements of the Confederate attack. Leaving Harrisburg at 2 P.M., the flotilla approached Morgan's Point at dusk, where a rowboat left the shore and pulled hard for the Rebel vessels. On board was a courier bearing Magruder's final communiqué, which ended: "All is ready. The Rangers of the Prairie send greeting to the Rangers of the Sea." Three times Colonel Green read the lines aloud to his men, receiving a volley of cheers each time; as night fell, the boats paddled off into the darkness.

Magruder had briefed his naval commanders as follows: The land forces must initiate the attack. The cottonclads were to approach as close to the Federal fleet as possible without being detected and wait for firing from the island to begin at 1 A.M. on New Year's Day. Magruder also informed his officers that he would press the fight with or without the navy, but under no circumstances was the fleet to start the battle. He knew that without a landward distraction, the cottonclads would not last long against Renshaw's fleet.

By midnight, the naval squadron had reached Half Moon Shoals, the men of Sibley's Brigade anxious for their first fight as "horse-marines." Nothing in their New Mexico experience had prepared them for service aboard a ship. As the small fleet steamed closer to Galveston, the tension among the volunteers grew. A party of officers gathered in a stateroom aboard the *Bayou City* to discuss their chances. One of the men asked Major Smith if the cotton bales afforded any protection. The veteran steamboatman assured them that the Federals' large-bore solid shot, shell, and grapeshot would be barely slowed by the "armor." The only option was to close with the Yankee vessels before they fired. After this remark, Colonel Green, now with a new concern for his soldiers' welfare, became decidedly serious. The men, perhaps sensing his fears, grew even more nervous. On deck, Colorado County privates Tom Kindred and Bill Cribbs went below and shuffled their playing cards for what they supposed was their last game of "seven up."

William Read Scurry: born Tennessee 1821; moved to Texas in 1837 and settled in San Augustine; enlisted as a private in the 2d Texas Mounted Volunteers at the outbreak of the Mexican War; after gallant service and promotion to major, he was mustered out at Monterey; appointed in 1859 commissioner to adjust the Texas-New Mexico boundary; known as an orator and a poet, he earned the title "Dirty Shirt" because of the road-grime on his garments; a member of the secession convention of 1861, he entered Confederate service as lieutenant colonel of the 4th

Texas Cavalry; participating in the New Mexico Campaign of General H.H. Sibley, Colonel Scurry commanded the 4th Texas in action both at Val Verde, where the regiment lost half its horses, and at Glorieta Pass, where he was a hero; promoted to full colonel just after Glorieta, with orders to return immediately to Texas and raise his own regiment, Scurry refused to leave until his men had time to write letters that he could take home with him; he told them it was like leaving "wife and children to take leave of us who had fought with him so brave-ly," noted a soldier. "He shed tears as he bade the men farewell. Thus we lost the best officer, most polished gentleman, most sociable gentleman, and most popular Colonel in the whole outfit."

Promoted to brigadier general in 1862, Scurry commanded the land forces during General John B. Magruder's recapture of Galveston in January 1863 and performed "with skill and gallantry" the "delicate duty" of withdrawing artillery from close proximity with the enemy; Magruder was so impressed that he recommended Scurry for promotion to major general, but promotion never came; Magruder nevertheless assigned Scurry to command Eastern Texas, where he constructed defensive fortifications at Galveston and on the Sabine River, sent several cavalry regiments to north Texas to patrol the Indian frontier and to apprehend deserters, and moved with what remained of his forces to Niblett's Bluff to check a possible Federal invasion of Texas; in September 1863 General E. Kirby Smith ordered Scurry to assume command of a brigade in General John G. Walker's Division, which was serving in Louisiana under General Richard Taylor; remaining in Louisiana, Scurry reported in March 1864 the beginning of General N.P. Banks's Red River Campaign; noting that four gunboats were "landing troops at Simsport," he stated: "I have advanced to the works and will try to check their advance. Troops in fine spirits and moving down handsomely." After leading his brigade in action at both Mansfield and Pleasant Hill, Scurry's command was transferred to Arkansas to oppose Federal General Frederick Steele's advance; at the Battle of Jenkins' Ferry, in April 1864, Scurry was mortally wounded; refusing to be taken to the rear, where surgeons might have saved his life, he bled to death on the battlefield; he is buried in the Texas State Cemetery at Austin. General Thomas N. Waul characterized him as the "gallant and daring Scurry."

6
"ALL THE STEAM YOU CAN CRACK ON!"

Magruder's plan quickly went awry as Yankee lookouts spied the approaching Rebel ships and, weighing anchor and building steam, quickly prepared for battle. Around 1 A.M., after the Confederate steamboats took a position near the west end of Pelican Island, a number of signal rockets streaked skyward from the *Harriet Lane*. Lanterns swung in the rigging—white for "enemy in sight," red for "make ready for action," blue for "order to prayers." On Kuhn's Wharf signal flares burned in response; inside the warehouse, drummers beat the long roll alerting the command to danger as the infantry scrambled to take their positions.

The *Bayou City* and *Neptune* hove to as their captains held a council of war. Commodore Smith, in view of his orders, decided not to risk starting the engagement and commanded his squadron withdrawn four miles to Half-Moon Shoals. The Union flagship U.S.S. *Westfield* steamed past Point Bolivar in an attempt to block the retreat of the Rebel ships. Galveston Bay was treacherously shallow, however, and the *Westfield*, true to its reputation, soon ran into trouble as it grounded on the shoals around Pelican Spit, near the city. Unable to back off of the sand bar, the commander signaled to the U.S.S. *Clifton* for aid.

Isaac Burrell's Massachusetts troops were alert and ready for the fight. During the day, the Colonel and Commander Wainwright had patrolled the streets of town and had witnessed troops drilling near Eagle Grove. Sensing danger, the naval officer had turned to Burrell and said, "Active operations going on colonel; things look squally, and we had better not remain here." As the group retreated, Wainwright added, "I will go up tomorrow and feel of them." That evening after sunset, the Union men had listened to artillery wheels rumbling in the

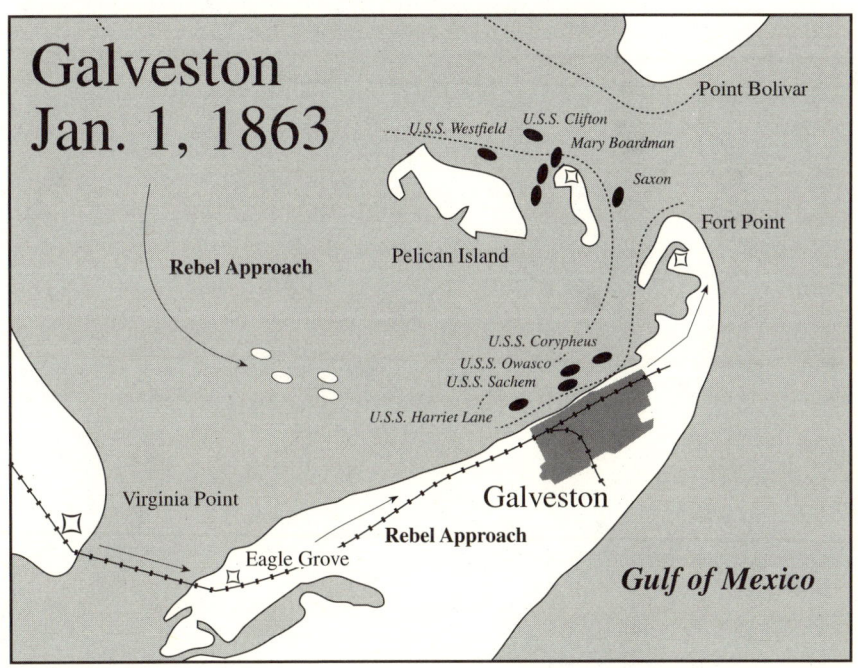

darkness, as well as the sounds of locomotives moving in the distance. Burrell arranged his men with the smoothbores of Company I on the right, the rifles of Company G on the left, and Company D in a perpendicular line in the middle, prepared to wheel toward the direction of any threat.

The Battle of Galveston began late, but in earnest, at 4 A.M. on New Year's Day with a flash of fire and smoke at the foot of 20th Street. As the gunboats had maneuvered in the bay, the land forces had crossed the railroad bridge from Virginia Point to the island. After taking positions, General Magruder had pulled the lanyard of one of Captain Tom Gonzales's field pieces to fire the signal round, before retiring to his headquarters at Broadway and Twenty-Fourth street. "I have done my part as a private," he remarked. "I will go and attend to that of general."

The Federal guns quickly thundered in reply. The U.S.S. *Harriet Lane* opened up an intense fire upon the Rebels at the west end of The Strand, discharging naval grapeshot that turned the ship's big cannon into devastating shotguns. Disintegrating shrapnel rounds showered the Confederate positions with whistling slugs; the U.S.S. *Corypheus* and U.S.S. *Sachem* added to the commotion with broadside after broadside tearing into the Confederate positions near Kuhn's Wharf.

At the Ursuline Convent, Dr. George Cupples of Magruder's staff prepared a hospital for the care of the wounded. "The heavens were in a blaze," he reported. "Musketry and heavy guns... roaring, rushing, and finally exploding in the air or on the vessels... The wounded began to come in very soon afterward."

Four miles away, Commodore Smith ordered his ships to action, yelling down the tube to the engine room, "Give me all the steam you can crack on!" The fleet gained speed as pipes hissed with high-pressure steam, the men of the naval expedition looking with amazement at the spectacle unfolding before them. Reports of the heavy guns shook the bay; bursting shells lighted for a brief moment the rigging of the enemy ships; burning fuses made graceful arcs through the air. Muffled explosions from the city streets and the sound of crashing debris added to the hellish cacophony.

On Kuhn's Wharf, the Massachusetts infantry began to receive the Rebel attack. Yankee pickets fired at the shadowy figures advancing down The Strand, then turned and ran desperately across the single plank to the safety of the barricades beyond. Troops hurriedly moved the sacks of cottonseed into the gap and took cover when round after round came screaming overhead. Two men flew back in a heap as a solid twelve-pound ball crashed through the plaster barrels. The warehouse disintegrated as bullets, canister, and cannonballs splintered the wood.

Burrell's troops took precautions to save themselves. While all of the troops lay flat, their commander continued to inspire. "The colonel walked the wharf, taking careful notice of all that occurred," wrote one Union veteran. "Many shells would drop upon the wharf and explode, or burst overhead, pieces flying forward and overboard, yet he did not receive a scratch." A shell crashed into the warehouse, setting it on fire. While some soldiers fought the blaze, throwing flaming tent canvas into the water, Burrell yelled for others to "come in here and rout out this ammunition." His quick action saved the command from a disastrous explosion.

In the city, the column of Rebel foot soldiers from the 4th, 5th, and 7th regiments advanced down Broadway toward their assigned objectives. The soldiers had gained the center of town when gunners from the U.S.S. *Owasco* detected their movements. Lieutenant Commander John Guest ordered *Owasco's* batteries to open fire and a number of heavy rounds passed only a few feet above the column as the troops surged forward. Rushing for cover, Colonel Reily led his troops behind the safety of the customs house as three well-aimed rounds quickly put holes through the building. Private William

Randolph Howell of the 5th Texas Cavalry wrote his sweetheart that "bombs, balls, grape, and canisters were flying all around and above me tearing up the earth, smashing up houses and killing and wounding men while the whole atmosphere seemed to be in a blaze. If I had consulted my personal safety, I should have preferred being somewhere else."

On Kuhn's Wharf, the Massachusetts men huddled under cover, hoping for good results from the navy. When the Rebel fire did not seem to slacken, one captain left his position and stood near the edge of the dock, hollering to the gunners aboard the *Sachem*. "Fire lower, and not so high!" Amazingly, the sailors heard the request over the din of battle and responded promptly and accurately.

As a result, the Confederate situation along The Strand rapidly deteriorated. The iron storm coming from the fleet silenced section after section of the Rebel artillery. On Twenty-First Street, Lieutenant Sidney Sherman, Jr., of Company A, 1st Texas Heavy Artillery, son of a famous Texas patriot, had his belly torn open by a piece of grapeshot. "A fine young fellow," Dr. Cupples reported as the boy was carried into the convent. "He died in an hour." Elsewhere, Dr. S.A.W. Fischer fell dead while attending the wounded, a piece of grapeshot having passed through his head, temple to temple. The largest Confederate cannon, the eight-inch "railway ram," lay abandoned. While inflicting some damage on the Federal fleet, the Rebel gunners had suffered appalling casualties.

John Guest: became a midshipman in the U.S. Navy in 1837; passed midshipman 1843; promoted to master and then to lieutenant in 1850; promoted successively to commander in 1862; to captain in 1866; and to commodore in 1872; Guest died in 1879.

Nearby, Colonel Cook's storming party had run into trouble on Eighteenth Street. The untried men of the 20th and 21st Texas had broken for cover several times and the veteran 2d Texas knew better than to attempt such a foolish assault. At 5 A.M., after wading just a few feet into the water with their ladders, the mass of wet, frightened men came under fire. "Captain Proctor sang out that he could see moving objects in the water," a sergeant in 42nd Massachusetts reported. "A volley was given, followed up by some rapid firing at will, as fast as the men could load. Those in the front ranks had to look out, for in the excitement men from the rear would crawl up and blaze away, regardless of friend or foe."

Although most of the inexperienced Bay State men fired high, their shots and cannon fire from the *Sachem* and *Corypheus* forced Cook's command out of the water and behind the slight shelter of a plank fence. In desperation, Confederate soldiers pushed one of Captain Tom Gonzales's guns forward and temporarily enfiladed the Kuhn's Wharf position, allowing Cook time to rush his men to the relative safety of a nearby cotton press. Unused scaling ladders bobbing in the water, along with a few bodies, marked the high tide of the Texan assault.

The Confederate attack on Galveston looked like a dismal failure. Increasing numbers of soldiers left their posts to escape the hail of canister and grape; hundreds scurried for the Gulf shore and the causeway. Magruder ordered a detachment of Xavier DeBray's 26th Texas Cavalry to round up the timid; orders were issued to shoot any soldier who resisted. With no signs of the Confederate naval flotilla, Magruder felt certain that the barrage would slaughter even more men come daylight, and he began making plans to end the attack. Just before dawn, he ordered Scurry to withdraw the remaining crews and guns from The Strand while details from Sibley's brigade retrieved any abandoned ordnance. Sunrise found few Rebels along The Strand and the Federal ships began to slacken the intense bombardment.

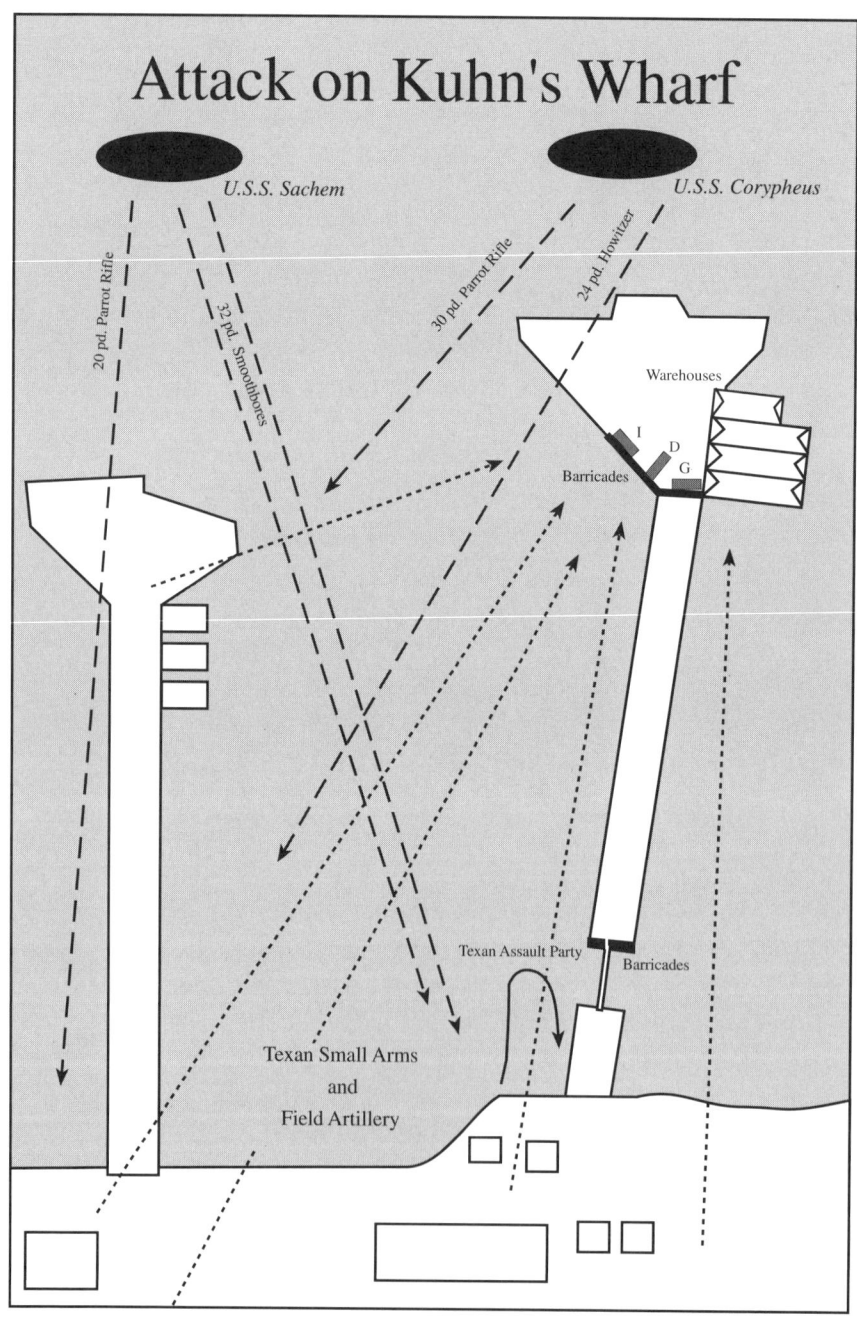

Attack on Kuhn's Wharf

U.S.S. Sachem

U.S.S. Corypheus

20 pd. Parrot Rifle

32 pd. Smoothbores

30 pd. Parrot Rifle

24 pd. Howitzer

Warehouses

I

D

G

Barricades

Texan Assault Party

Barricades

Texan Small Arms
and
Field Artillery

As dawn slowly broke, a few Texan riflemen and gunners renewed a steady pelting of Kuhn's Wharf, eliciting return fire. A Rebel field piece placed in the foundry nearby began lobbing shells among the Federals. "Some shells...exploded underneath the wharf, making it a question whether the piling would not eventually be severed," the Union sergeant remembered. "The gunners had also got the range where the men lay, and by a little elevation they could sweep them." Burrell called for volunteers to quiet the Texan gun; a few well-placed sharpshooters silenced the cannon. Burrell then ordered a detachment to take a skiff laying on the wharf and attempt to communicate with the fleet. As volunteers slid the boat into the water, it immediately filled and sank from a dozen undiscovered bullet holes.

This cluster of Union men and officers brought sniper fire from the town. "As the bullets began to whistle over their heads the men shouted 'Look out, colonel, they are firing at you!'" One private clutched his hand, a bullet having passed clean through. Others took cover behind posts while the commander of the 42nd took advantage of a freight gangway to slide out of slight. After cannons from the U.S.S. *Owasco* silenced the pesky Rebels, Burrell emerged waving, telling his men, "I am all right."

The Union forces began to feel easy about their situation. Riflemen kept abandoned Confederate cannon in their sights, shooting at the occasional Rebels attempting to carry the guns off. Naval gunners periodically lobbed shells into suspected sharpshooter positions.

Burrell decided to take the initiative. "Volunteers were called for, to go out and ascertain the position of the enemy," the Union sergeant continued. "The selection fell upon Private Colson, Company I, a rather tough customer who had been put in irons for misbehavior...but been released." The miscreant turned hero scampered across the plank to the mainland only to return in a hurry. The Texans, although temporarily quieted,

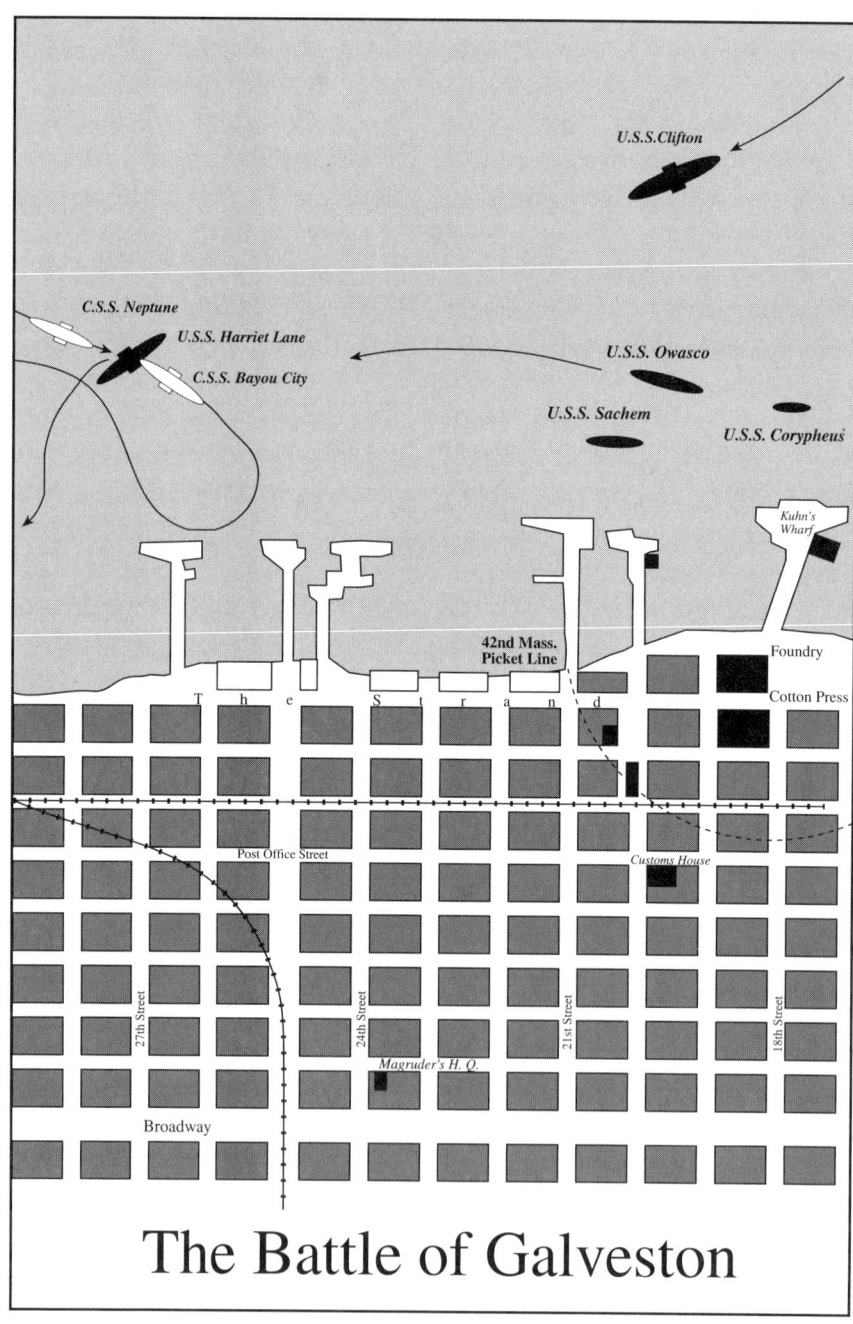

The Battle of Galveston

remained close by. As though to reassure the nervous Union land forces, naval vessels drew in close to the wharf to aid the Massachusetts infantry in discovering Magruder's next move. The *Harriet Lane*, its maneuvering room limited, had reversed its wheels and begun backing down the line of wharves fronting the harbor. *Owasco* and *Clifton* also approached.

While the Union navy probed the vicinity of Kuhn's Wharf, a spontaneous, hopeful cheer echoed from the shore as the looked-for Rebel steamers finally appeared through the smoke and early morning haze, pressing an attack. The Confederate paddle wheelers, "puffing and snorting from their high pressure steam," according to one Texan sharpshooter, churned through the bay as their cannon roared at the Federal ships. The second round from the *Bayou City* hit just behind the *Harriet Lane's* port wheel, "making a hole large enough for a man to crawl through" according to one observer. Before other shots could be brought to bear, however, the refitted thirty-two-pounder aboard *Bayou City* burst, killing Wier and several of his men.

At the sound of renewed activity, observers in town ran to discover the source. "I went up to the third story to see our boats attacking," wrote Dr. Cupples. "It was a splendid slight, the blaze of musketry incessant and the vessels and water looking like Stereoscopic views."

Slightly ahead, the *Bayou City* drove bow-on for the *Harriet Lane* which by now was reversing its engine for a forward thrust. Sharpshooters drove the Yankee crew from the deck of the Union gunboat as Captain Lubbock ordered his pilot to close with the enemy vessel, ramming it if possible, so that it could be taken by boarding. Instead, the *Bayou City* struck only a glancing blow to the oncoming ship. A portion of the cottonclad's port wheel house was smashed by the *Harriet Lane's* bow while, at the same time, a portion of the Union ship's anchoring apparatus sheared away, causing the hook and fifteen fathoms of cable to slide into the water, slowing the

Union vessel's progress to a crawl. Confederate crewmen quickly dropped the port boarding plank; the intervening angle caused the board to fall into the water and rip free, catching in the wheel of *Bayou City* and causing further damage. The crippled Confederate steamboat quickly abandoned the assault

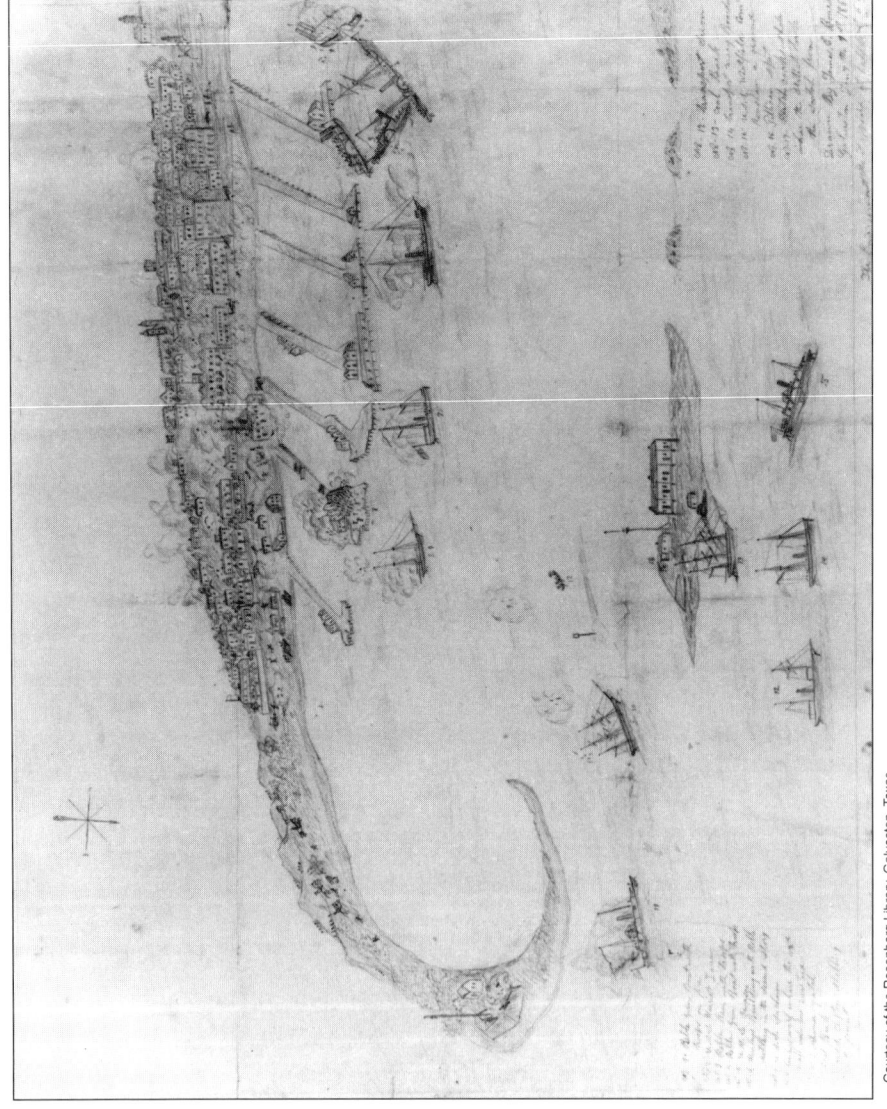

The Battle of Galveston, a primitive drawing made, apparently, by an eyewitness

and ran past its target toward the shore as the Yankee sailors hurried back to their guns. In the confusion of the assault, the *Harriet Lane* had also run its bow into the mud.

Meanwhile, Captain William Sangster of the *Neptune* ordered his ship to finish off the *Harriet Lane*, now anchored and aground. "We had two 24-pounders on board that roared with extraordinary loud report," remembered Joseph Faust. As the Rebel ship cut to port in an effort to gain a better angle on the maneuvering Union gunboat, a shot from the *Harriet Lane* scattered *Neptune's* cotton bales and lumber, sending lethal splinters flying among the crew. "We then opened a frightful rifle-fire on them just as a bomb exploded in our midst and hit many," Faust reported. He, and many of his fellow Germans, became casualties. "H. Sippel dead, and R. Haas seriously wounded. Sylvester Simon, Wilhelm Simon, Fritz Penshorn also were hit by splinters but only slightly. I was hit on the chest by a wood splinter and sank unconscious to the floor." Gaining momentum, the wounded *Neptune* closed the distance and slammed hard into the side of the Yankee ship, ten feet behind her starboard paddle wheel.

The men of the 7th Texas Cavalry fired quickly at the Union vessel as sailors tried unsuccessfully to grapple and secure their prize. Amidst the maelstrom, Union Commander Wainwright fell seriously wounded. *Neptune*, however, was in trouble. The rest of the Federal fleet, especially the U.S.S. *Owasco*, began to find the range, hurling round after round at the Rebel riverboat. With water pouring in through her mangled bow, and the surface of the bay churning from enemy cannon fire, the sinking vessel backed away from the *Harriet Lane* and headed for the shallows off Thirty-Second Street. As *Neptune* retreated, a point blank shot from one of the *Lane's* IX-inch Dahlgrens blew a huge hole in the cottonclad's bow, causing it to quickly founder.

With one ship sinking and the other crippled, the Confederate naval attack, like its shore-side counterpart, seemed a total loss. "A round of cheers went up on board the *Harriet Lane,* and her men threw their caps into the air with joy, supposing all was ended," a Union veteran remembered.

However, the Rebel sailors were determined to make another dash at the Federal ship before accepting defeat. The crew of the *Bayou City* cleared its damaged wheel of debris, and turned the vessel around. Captain Lubbock's steamer gained speed as the *Harriet Lane's* crew returned to their battle stations and attempted to haul in the anchor and back off the shoal to safety. One Yankee gun crew managed to fire a last round at the onrushing cottonclad, sending a solid shot through its wheel house without effect. Meanwhile, sharpshooters aboard the stricken *Neptune* renewed their firing even as salt water rushed across its lowest deck. This pelting from small arms scattered the Yankee blue jackets, allowing the *Bayou City* to finish her run. A deafening crash and tremendous jolt signaled the impact as the ship drove into the port paddle wheel of the Federal vessel. Deck debris tumbled to the right as the stricken ship heeled over from the collision, groaning timbers buckling and breaking as the twisted wheel braces of *Harriet Lane* impaled the Confederate steamer, locking the antagonists together.

Now, the Rebel soldiers finished their work as they boarded the Federal ship. Major Smith, cutlass in hand, appeared on the bow of the *Bayou City,* hurried over to the Yankee ship's netting, and began to cut it free. Clambering over the rail, he looked back and called for his men to follow. Smith then turned and shot Union Commander J.M. Wainwright through the forehead at close range as the Rebel gun crew and sharpshooters rushed forward, downing the rest of the net as they tumbled onto the deck of the *Harriet Lane.* The steamer was strangely silent; signs of the deadly fusillade were everywhere. The Yankee skipper lay dead; besides the bullet in his head, three others had ripped his frock coat, and three pierced his thigh. The executive officer, Lieutenant Commander Edward

Lea, with five bullets in his abdomen, was dying. Three other crewmen, two with head wounds and another with his belly peppered by buckshot, lay sprawled and motionless. Quietly, a Federal sailor stepped out from behind a door, held up his hands, and surrendered the ship. "The pride of the Yankee Navy," crowed Dr. Cupples, "was the prize of our Cow-boys."

The booming of artillery began anew as Union ship commanders realized what had happened and made an attempt to recapture the *Harriet Lane*. The U.S.S. *Owasco*, its bow cannon already firing vigorously, steamed along the row of wharves and turned slightly to starboard, one half-mile from the Rebel ships. A powerful XI-inch Dahlgren amidships, already the bane of the men on shore, pivoted and hurled shells screeching toward the captured vessel, one smashing a sizable hole in the *Harriet Lane's* stern.

The Rebels scrambled for cover and began to combat this new threat and defend their prize. Gunners attempted to bring the *Harriet Lane's* cannon to bear, but failed because the ship was listing too greatly from the ram attack. Meanwhile, soldiers of Green's regiment abandoned their own ship for the presumed safety of the captured steamer. Furiously, Captain Lubbock asked Green to prevent the panicked men from deserting his ship. The Colonel succeeded in turning back half of them, who soon opened a rapid fire against the *Owasco*. As bullets whistled through that ship's rigging, one Texan noted that "the crowd of men on the *Owasco's* decks seemed to melt like snow under a summer's sun." The commander of the Federal ship, his gun crews falling around him, quickly ordered his engines reversed and backed out of range of the deadly Rebel Enfields.

As the *Owasco* retreated, it passed within thirty feet of Kuhn's Wharf. "She was hailed by Colonel Burrell to take his men off," a Union participant recalled, "The request was heard on board, but no response given. The *Owasco* kept on."

Quiet settled over the bay as the opposing forces arranged a truce and considered the implications of the capture of the

Capture of the U.S.S *Harriet Lane*

Harriet Lane. A white flag hung from the stern of the captured ship and Captain Lubbock, a daring bluff in mind, ordered a boat and crew to row him toward the enemy fleet. Upon being taken aboard U.S.S. *Owasco,* he boldly demanded the surrender of the remaining Union vessels, giving the Federals three hours to decide.

While awaiting the outcome of this stratagem, the Rebels were busy attempting to separate their tangled ships. Officers and men of the Confederate flotilla struggled to disengage the *Bayou City* from its victim. The *John F. Carr,* held in reserve during the battle, attempted to tow the cottonclad away, but without success. In desperation, the steamboat dragged the two combatant vessels to the Twenty-Seventh Street Wharf where men from Green's regiment attempted to rock the boats apart by gathering on the bow. Rebel officers soon concluded that the services of several carpenters and skilled mechanics would be required to untangle the mess.

Union Commodore Renshaw, shaken by the sudden change in fortune, agreed to Lubbock's outlandish demands and ordered white flags run up on his fleet for the duration of the three hour truce. He then sent for his ship's officers and held a council of war. The men of the 42d Massachusetts watched helplessly as the hard fighting *Sachem* and *Corypheus* left their posts and headed toward Pelican Spit.

With the cease-fire underway, soldiers, surgeons, and hospital stewards began their bloody work of gathering and tending the wounded. Near Kuhn's Wharf, a dozen Rebel casualties from the scaling ladder expedition awaited stretchers. Along The Strand, artillerymen with a wide variety of gory wounds awaited treatment. Confused clusters of men wandered aimlessly about, looking for friends among the injured. Horse-drawn ambulances clattered along, stopping at various points to load more casualties. A burial detail on the tip of the island closed up the hole they had hastily dug for a member of their company.

Twenty-four hours after they had parted, the "Rangers of the Sea" were finally reunited with the "Rangers of the Prairie" as brigade casualties were counted. At the Twenty-Seventh Street Wharf, soldiers from the 5th Texas Cavalry carried friends from the *Bayou City*, placing them beside comrades wounded in the city streets. Nineteen-year-old John Hogsett had received his first wound at Val Verde, New Mexico. He had later been captured and then paroled. Now, he took a stretcher ride to the Ursuline Convent. Lieutenant J.H. Alexander of Palestine had also been wounded at Val Verde, but as a private. Now, after three promotions and an outstanding military career, he was to be buried. Aboard the *Neptune*, the bodies of eight men from Anderson County, over half of the volunteer squad from Company I, 7th Texas Cavalry, were being put into boats to be carried to shore. Thirty-three men had been killed or wounded in that regiment, most of them while attacking the *Harriet Lane*. "The wounds, being mostly from Shells, Splinters, and Grape shot, are unusually dangerous," noted Dr. Cupples.

For the Union infantry, the situation appeared hopeless. A soldier appeared on the breastwork with a strip of sail cloth tied to an oar. Others fixed handkerchiefs to bayonets and ramrods. Colonel Burrell, from behind his barricades on Kuhn's Wharf, asked for some time to communicate with the vessels of the fleet. Confederate officers agreed, allowing him a half-hour to accomplish his mission. Burrell sent a single officer by rowboat to ask Renshaw to save his men, but that man never returned. Meanwhile, Texans could be seen moving closer to the wharf and putting their field guns back into position to rake the Federal line. When time expired, Burrell surrendered.

Rebels moved quickly to accept. General Scurry arrived first, but gallantly refused Burrell's sword. At the same time, yelling Texans mobbed the wharf, disarming their enemy and asking their prisoners scores of questions regarding the number of men killed and the intensity of the fight. The commander of the Confederate forces then made his appearance. "When Major General Magruder, in a gorgeous uniform, met Colonel Burrell, he remarked 'Don't be cast down, colonel, it is the fortunes of war,'" reported the Union sergeant. "You will soon be paroled." Besides weapons and equipment, the colors of the 42nd Massachusetts fell into Texan hands.

With the threat of hostilities resuming momentarily, Confederate soldiers hurried the Union prisoners into town and away from the expected danger. At Kuhn's Wharf, the 240 men of the 42nd Massachusetts emerged from behind their solid barricades and marched down The Strand in a column of fours, Colonel Burrell in the lead. Confederate surgeons and Yankee privates removed a half-dozen blue-coated casualties, loading them into waiting carriages. Amazingly, none of the Bay State men had been killed. Companies from the 20th Texas Infantry, tired and shaken after their first exposure to battle, stood in line of battle as the Yankee soldiers passed. A similar column marched up Twenty-Seventh Street as the dejected crewman from the *Harriet Lane* were escorted away.

Aboard the *Westfield*, an amazing rumor, circulating through the fleet for days, identified the *Bayou City* as an casemated ironclad ram. Renshaw, whose crewmen included veterans from the U.S.S. *Congress*—which had felt the wrath of the C.S.S. *Virginia* off Hampton Roads—issued orders designed to save the rest of his command from a similar fate. Regardless of the Rebels' so-called truce, Renshaw ordered his vessels to sea at once. By mid-morning, the Federal ships began to gather speed and made a dash for the mouth of Galveston Bay, white flags still streaming from their masts.

U.S.S. *Westfield*, still hard aground, could not be saved. Renshaw, after seeing to the safety of his fleet, ordered his flagship destroyed. Crewmen rapidly splashed turpentine and gunpowder below decks and prepared a slow match. Undoubtedly with pangs of remorse, Renshaw left the ill-starred old ferryboat to its fate, twelve blue jackets straining at the oars of one of the ship's whaleboats heading for the transport *Saxon*. After reaching a safe distance, the bulk of *Westfield's* crew continued on to the safety of an awaiting transport while Renshaw and his detachment paused to await the flagship's demise. Nothing occurred. Furious, Renshaw ordered the launch to return to the *Westfield*, demanding that this time the job be done correctly. As the launch drew alongside, Renshaw leapt aboard his abandoned ship. At the same moment, the forward magazines erupted, obliterating the Commodore and his shamefaced crew. Debris showered the area—a revolver landed among the Confederates in Galveston. Little was left of the *Westfield*, just some twisted machinery and its shattered, smoking hull. The flagship, its commander, and twelve crewmen had died together.

As the muffled explosion rumbled from Pelican Spit the rest of the Union fleet escaped to sea. Alarmed at this truce violation, Rebel artillerymen, desperate to stop the enemy vessels, hurried back to their posts and began to unlimber guns. The occasional booming of cannon grew increasingly regular and intense as Rebel gunners tried unsuccessfully to halt the Yankee flight.

The Rebels were determined to capture the rest of the fleet, and Commodore Smith ordered all available ships to pursue. Men from Sibley's brigade, milling by the Twenty-Seventh Street Wharf, were called aboard the *John F. Carr* as that steamer cast off and gathered steam. The unarmored Rebel paddle wheeler, adding more fuel to its fires, attempted to build as much speed as possible; the last of the Union ships, however, amidst water churned by Confederate guns firing from the beach, had already safely passed over the bar at the mouth of the harbor. The Rebel commander reluctantly ended the chase as the Gulf breakers splashed over the boat's lower deck, and the crew of the *John F. Carr* returned to the bay. Six hours after it had started, the Battle of Galveston was over.

In their haste the Federals had abandoned several vessels intact, and the crew of the *John F. Carr* took inventory. Near the edge of the city, Confederate sailors boarded the captured schooner *Lecompte* and posted a guard. A mile further east along the island, the supply boat *Cavallo*, loaded with coal and general merchandise, surrendered, her three-man crew and a government contract merchant offering no resistance. The *John F. Carr* then approached Pelican Spit where the shattered hulk of the *Westfield*, its weaponry intact, still burned along the waterline. Here, as the U.S.S. *Sachem* fired harmless long-range shots from the Gulf, the crew of the Rebel steamboat grappled the anchored supply ship *Elias Pike* and sent aboard a crew. These would be the only additional prizes that day.

The battle had been intense, and on shore surgeons and first sergeants from both armies started the task of counting their casualties. Sibley's Brigade had lost seventeen men killed and twenty-eight wounded, some later dying. The other Confederate forces engaged lost ten men killed and another one hundred wounded. Federal gunfire killed one civilian in the city, and wounded two volunteer sailors from Houston. Besides the thirteen killed from the *Westfield*, five Union sailors died aboard the *Harriet Lane*, and an additional twelve were wounded. Sixteen sailors became casualties aboard the *Owasco*. Two other blue jackets suffered wounds, one each aboard the *Clifton* and *Sachem*.

The devastation in Galveston was apparent. Large-caliber cannon balls littered the streets. Unexploded rounds lay half-buried in the dirt; furrows from solid shot cut across the boulevards. Grapeshot and pieces of shell covered the ground. Spent bullets were everywhere, especially around Kuhn's Wharf. Field artillery pieces also rested amid the rubble. Limbers and guns sat idle, hidden behind walls and in hedges where their crews or men from Sibley's Brigade had dragged them. Buildings along The Strand were demolished. For blocks into the city, naval artillery had knocked frame houses to pieces, scattering the debris across the streets. The U.S. customs house, completed in 1860 but never occupied, had several new holes. Projectiles had completely scarred and mangled Perry's Foundry and the Merchants Cotton Press and sheds, where Colonel Cook's storming party had sought refuge, having been the object of much Federal attention.

Aboard the *Harriet Lane*, though, incidents had occurred that were poignant reminders of the tragedy of the war. In the mélee, one of the Texan boarders had grabbed an enemy sailor by the throat, demanding his surrender. "Look me in the face," the Federal had said. Upon doing so, the Texan recognized his own brother. In another family tragedy, the *Harriet Lane's* executive officer, Lieutenant Commander Edward Lea, lay dying on deck. His father, Alfred M. Lea, was on shore, serving as a major of engineers on Magruder's staff. Hearing of his son's distress, the elder Lea sought an ambulance to carry his boy to a hospital; before the conveyance could be located, the boy expired, breathing out the words "my father is here" as he died.

7

TRAITORS, WOMEN, AND LIQUOR

On the morning after the battle, the importance of the Confederate victory became obvious when a Federal steamer, *Cambria*, with Colonel Edmund Jackson Davis and his Federal 1st Texas Cavalry aboard, as well as arms and equipment to raise another regiment, appeared in the Gulf. With Galveston as a base, Yankee soldiers would then have been free to raid the interior, and the city's repair and dock facilities would have served to tighten the blockade along the Texas coast. With supplies dwindling in the state, and the enemy driving deep into the heartland, pro-Union Germans and disaffected Anglos might have swelled Davis's ranks and forced Confederate authorities to bring home a substantial number of Texas troops serving on other fronts. The infusion of 1,000 more Yankee rifles in the streets of the city might have prevented the Rebels from winning, keeping Galveston in Union control.

Magruder decided to lure the *Cambria* into the bay and capture the entire renegade Union regiment. Rebel sailors hoisted the United States flag aboard the *Harriet Lane* and another topped the customs house to give the appearance that Galveston was still under Union control. The Yankee ship lowered a boat and dispatched men to find a harbor pilot willing to guide them, but the Confederates captured these sailors

Edmund J. Davis: born Florida 1827; moved with his widowed mother to Texas in 1838 settling first in Galveston; studied law in Corpus Christi and later practiced in Laredo, Corpus Christi, and Brownsville; served as deputy collector of customs with headquarters at Laredo from 1850 to 1852; elected district attorney at Brownsville in 1853, and made judge of the district from 1854 to 1861, which included all of the Texas portion of the lower Rio Grande Valley; he held that position until he was defeated for election to the Secession Convention at the outbreak of the Civil War; his friends attributed to that defeat his alienation from the Confederate cause; he organized a regiment of cavalry composed mainly of Unionists who had escaped from Texas into Mexico and, while recruiting for his regiment near Matamoros, was captured by a band of Confederates and narrowly escaped hanging; his regiment spent most of the war period in Louisiana, but Davis led the unsuccessful Union attack on Laredo in 1864; he was made a brigadier general of U.S. volunteers in November 1864; a delegate to the Texas constitutional convention of 1866 and president of the convention of 1869; among other proposals, he adovcated unrestricted black suffrage, the disfranchisement of some ex-Confederates, and the division of Texas into more  than one state; elected governor in 1869 with Federal military support, Davis exercised great power for the duration of his term, for example, having authority to appoint over eight thousand state and local employees; ousted by a majority of forty thousand Democratic votes in 1873, he appealed unsuccessfully to President U.S. Grant to be sustained in office; Davis then resumed his law practice in Austin, Texas, where he died in 1883; he is buried in the State Cemetery.

when the launch reached the wharf. They then recrewed the boat and rowed back to try to lead the enemy ship into the bay. Volunteers from Sibley's Brigade were immediately called for maritime duty, this time to man the *Harriet Lane*. Since this ship proved to be still disabled, the troops transferred to one of the captured sailing vessels. By the time the excited Rebels had reached the bar, however, the crew of the *Cambria* had discovered the identity of the bogus pilot boat and steamed back to sea.

After the excitement of the past few days, life in camp became increasingly dull for the men of Sibley's Brigade. One of the sailors captured in the Union pilot boat was a deserter from Colonel Cook's regiment known as Thomas "Nicaragua" Smith. His execution on January 8, 1863, was well attended. "He was taken from jail with music and brought out to a vacant piece of land nearby where the entire military was standing in rank and file," Joseph Faust, recovering from his wounds, wrote home. "He was stood up before his jury, would not have his eyes blindfolded, so then he was shot by a twelve-man squad." Later that week, Commodore Smith issued another call for sailors and a number of the brigade responded; when the *Harriet Lane* underwent her test run, the repairs were obviously still not complete.

Also on January 8, the blockade of Galveston resumed with the arrival of a new Union flotilla fresh from Pensacola and Mobile led by Commodore Henry H. Bell aboard the twenty-four-gun screw steamer U.S.S. *Brooklyn*. In company with that vessel were the five-gun side-wheeler U.S.S. *Hatteras*, the screw schooner *New London*, and three "Ninety-Day Gunboats," the *Sciota*, *Cayuga*, and *Owasco*. For the following two days, the ships shelled the newly erected forts guarding the beach, but with little effect.

As Sibley's Brigade settled back into camp near the railroad depot, participants began to criticize their conduct in the battle. Those aboard the cottonclads felt superior to their land bound comrades, and many suggested that the Sibley Brigade troops on shore were cowards and had panicked along with the green artillerymen. Even Colonel Reily's ability as a commander came into question. The second-guessing and finger-pointing, however, became general as even Green's men aboard the *Bayou City* came under criticism. In the heat of battle and after the ramming had occurred, the men of the 5th Texas, accusations correctly asserted, had abandoned their vessel to seek refuge below deck in the *Harriet Lane*.

There was no doubt, too, that many of the Texans had irrefutably and shamelessly plundered their fellow soldiers. Although many had been issued new weapons, some supplemented their arsenal with fourteen additional Enfields and several articles of clothing stolen from the gun crew of the *Bayou City*. When Captain Lubbock left his ship during the battle to arrange the truce, he left his shotgun and a brace of pistols behind; these, too, disappeared.

U.S.S. _Brooklyn_

Despite the minor tarnishes on its reputation, Sibley's Brigade also shared in the glory of the fight. Although their ship sank, the men aboard the *Neptune*, because of their devastating and constant firing, received credit from some for the successful sea attack. Magruder singled out Colonel Bagby for commendation in his official report, and Colonel Green, already well known for his service to the Republic of Texas and to the Confederacy, became one of the principal heroes of the Battle of Galveston, erasing much of the stain from New Mexico.

The men of Sibley's Brigade were a rowdy and ill-disciplined bunch, to be sure, but they had provided the Confederacy with the victory at Galveston by displaying a gallantry under unusual circumstances that had few parallels in the war. Unaccustomed to serving aboard ships, the men had enthusiastically volunteered for the hazardous duty, showing courage as they faced the enemy fleet. Those who served on land were steady soldiers, called on by Magruder to brave Federal fire and retrieve the ordnance abandoned by more fainthearted comrades. The men of the brigade had shown that despite their lack of traditional soldierly qualities, they were warriors, and could be counted on to be equal to any challenge.

More importantly, Sibley's Brigade was instrumental in delivering Galveston back to the Confederacy, a major contribution at that time. Although still blockaded, the harbor once again offered safe haven for the successful blockade runner. By war's end, it would be the most important port in the Confederacy. The recapture of the island, by denying the enemy a forward base of operations, also protected the vulnerable Texas interior from invasion.

Galveston also had symbolic implications. The morale of Texas troops in distant theaters was directly affected by affairs back home and the fall of the state's most important city had cast doubt on the government's ability to protect their wives and families. The Southern victory had also reversed the course of the war in that region, showing that the powerful Union navy was not invincible, and that daring and creative men could outmatch the enemy's warships. The victory had, in a dramatic way, returned hope to Texas.

The tangible symbols of the victory were welcome trophies. New cannon defended the Texas coast. Dockhands repaired newly acquired ships and would soon load on cotton for a dash to foreign ports. The Union prisoners, too, would remind Texans of their victory as most of the Yankee sailors and infantry would serve many months at Camp Groce near Hempstead and Camp Ford near Tyler. Fate was cruel for the handful of African-Americans captured in the fight. Two free blacks from Boston, having accompanied the 42nd Massachusetts as servants, found themselves auctioned off to two local planters. Confederates placed the black sailors from the *Harriet Lane* in irons and sent them to the state penitentiary at Huntsville as dangerous criminals.

But with no stirring deeds to be done in the maritime realm and with the lackluster bombardment barely a distraction, boredom soon took hold of the Rebel garrison, and they turned with abandon to the two standard troop entertainments, women and liquor.

A week after the battle, Lieutenant John Coleman of Falls County, Texas, along with a group of other officers from Sibley's Brigade, left camp and started "on a spree" that added to the loose-disciplined reputation of the Texas cavalrymen turned marines. Finding an untended carriage, which happened to be General Magruder's, the officers climbed in and headed for a house of "assignation" on the beach. When they arrived, however, the proprietress informed them that no women remained. Undaunted, the group searched the house, discovering no females but plenty of brandy, which they soon drank. As their party became louder, two neighbors thought that looters had broken into the house, and began shooting. The officers quickly left the building and approached the strangers. As one of the neighbors pulled his gun, Lieutenant Coleman fired a shot, grazing the man's head. Regaining his footing, the civilian tried to shoot again, prompting Coleman to send a second bullet into the citizen's shoulder. For this incident, the lieutenant was demoted and transferred out of the brigade into a conscript regiment.

After a few more weeks of inactivity on Galveston Island, the veterans of Sibley's Brigade received orders to march once again, preparatory to their next campaign. The brigade was to rejoin General Sibley, by now cleared of all misconduct charges, at New Iberia, Louisiana. On January 16, the troops left the city, their battle flags bearing the names "Galveston" and "Galveston Bay" beside those of "Val Verde" and "Glorieta."

8

"'Texan' a Better Word than 'Spartan'"

At his headquarters, Farragut was furious. The disaster at Galveston, he railed, was "the most melancholy affair ever recorded in the history of our gallant navy." He cursed the late Commodore Renshaw and moved to sack Captain R. L. Law of the *Clifton* for leaving the battle before properly relieved. He trusted Commodore Bell, on board the *Brooklyn*, to avoid such catastrophes in the future. Little did either man know that the Battle of Galveston was the first in a series of three January misfortunes for the United States Navy in Texas waters.

Captain Raphael Semmes of the commerce raider C.S.S. *Alabama*, his reputation for cunning and daring already well advanced, had heard rumors from blockade runners of some sort of action on the Texas coast to commence early in the year. After spending a half year preying on merchant men and whalers in the Atlantic, the C.S.S. *Alabama* had moved to the warmer climate of the Gulf of Mexico for the winter. Perusing a Boston newspaper, Semmes read of planned operations on the Texas Gulf Coast and saw an opportunity for the *Alabama* to serve as a regular ship-of-war instead of a commerce raider. Semmes had no idea that Magruder's battle was already over and won when he directed the *Alabama* to leave the Arcas Keys in the Gulf of Campeche and steam up the Texas coast in the second week of January.

In the late afternoon of January 11, Commodore Bell received news of an unidentified bark-rigged vessel cruising well off to sea. Preliminary indications were that the ship was a blockade runner making for Galveston, and he decided to investigate. He ordered Captain H.C. Blake of the U.S.S. *Hatteras* to sortie toward the mystery ship at sundown. As the Union warship moved to sea, the mystery ship turned and fled into moonless darkness.

The crew of the *Hatteras* believed that a midnight chase awaited them as they pursued the supposed merchant ship. The vessel's lines and rigging seemed to confirm it as indeed a swift, though

Richard L. Law: became a midshipman in the U.S. Navy in 1841; passed midshipman 1847; graduated from the U.S. Naval Academy in 1847 in the same class as Joseph J. Cook, a Confederate Colonel he would face a the Battle of Galveston; promoted first to master and then to lieutenant in 1855; promoted to lieutenant-commander in 1862; following the death of William Renshaw during the Battle of Galveston, January 1, 1863, Law took command of the Federal flotilla; he disengaged and withdrew his ships, leaving Galveston once again in Confederate hands; Law was promoted to commander in 1866 and to captain in 1877; he retired from the navy in 1886, and died in 1891.

Raphael Semmes: born Maryland 1809; began his naval career as a midshipman in 1826; during leaves he studied law and in 1834 was admitted to the Maryland bar; commissioned a lieutenant in 1837, Semmes commanded blockading vessels during the War with Mexico; when his ship, the *Somers*, sank, he barely escaped death; he authored two books on the war: *The Campaign of General Scott* and *Service Afloat and Ashore During the Mexican War*; in 1849 he moved to Mobile, Alabama, and became inspector of lighthouses along the Gulf Coast; promoted to commander in 1855 and placed in charge of the Navy Lighthouse Bureau, a position he held until 1861; Semmes resigned from the U.S. Navy soon after Alabama seceded; he first served the Confederacy by purchasing munitions and supplies in the North; after the war began, he became a commander in the Confederate Navy and assigned to head the Lighthouse Bureau; soon he received permission to convert the steamer, the *Havana*, into a commerce raider; renaming his ship the *Sumter* in June 1861, Semmes began a cruise of six months during which he captured eighteen prizes; Federal vessels eventually blockaded the *Sumter* in Gibraltar, but Semmes escaped to England and took command of the C.S.S. *Alabama*; promoted to captain in 1862, he sailed from England, roaming the oceans in search of prizes; in two years he captured sixty-nine vessels; the U.S.S. *Kearsage* finally sank the *Alabama* off Cherbourg, France, in 1864, but Semmes was rescued by a yacht and taken to England; returning to the Confederacy, he was promoted to rear admiral in February 1865 and placed in command of the James River Squadron; after Richmond fell, Semmes destroyed his ships and moved westward with his sailors; President Davis appointed "Old Beeswax," as his men called him, a brigadier general and directed him to defend Danville, Virginia; when Confederate forces surrendered, Semmes insisted that his parole list him both as a rear admiral and as a brigadier general; he emphasized that his army rank be included on his parole to prevent any attempt to try him as a naval "pirate" for his raiding activities; Semmes returned to Mobile after the war, briefly serving as county probate judge, but Reconstruction officials removed him from office; for a time he taught moral philosophy at the Louisiana Military Institute (later Louisiana State University) and edited a Memphis newspaper; he returned to Mobile in 1868 to practice law; he died in 1877 and is buried in the Mobile Catholic Cemetery.

Sinking of the U.S.S. *Hatteras* by the C.S.S. *Alabama*

badly handled, blockade runner. Although trimmly rigged, the runner seemed sluggish. After a few hours, the fugitive ship slowed to a stop some twenty miles from the rest of the Union fleet, its sails furled as though exhausted. *Hatteras* moved to within one hundred yards of the seemingly helpless vessel and lowered a boat and boarding party.

As the Union blue jackets closed the distance, a voice hailed them. "This is the Confederate States Steamer *Alabama*." Moments later, the Confederate vessel fired a crisp, devastating broadside.

The *Hatteras*, pummeled amidships, shuddered sideways in the water as the heavy rounds smashed though its port side. The *Hatteras* responded slowly to the ambush, and soon Confederate shot and shell carried away part of its engine and opened its hull to the sea. In thirteen minutes, the U.S.S. *Hatteras* was burning and adrift, its magazines flooded and many of its crew dead. Captain Blake ordered a gun fired to leeward and struck his colors. Boats from the *Alabama* dropped to the sea and moved to rescue some 118 survivors. Time was short, however, as the *Hatteras* slipped deeper into the Gulf. Within six minutes, the ship was gone. The *Alabama* had claimed its thirty-fifth victim at the cost of a carpenter's mate with a cheek wound. In Galveston that night, the citizens and garrison watched in wonder from the rooftops of the town as mysterious flashes lit the dark southwestern horizon.

On the morning of January 12, the *Brooklyn* and her consorts arrived at the scene of the previous night's action. Chunks of the *Hatteras* still floated on the waves. Extremely conscious that the shame of the navy had just been increased, the vessels returned to the monotonous shelling of Galveston. The *Alabama*, meanwhile, was 100 miles away sailing hard for Jamaica.

Three days later, far to the east, an unintended benefit of the fighting along the Texas coast manifested itself at Mobile, Alabama. With the West Gulf Blockading Squadron frantic and addled off Galveston, Commander John N. Maffit of the C.S.S.

Florida seized his chance to escape the blockade that had him bottled up in the bay. He had brought his raider through the blockade into Mobile four months earlier with yellow fever raging on board. Since that time, Union vessels had sealed him in port. After the *Brooklyn* and other vessels had been drawn off this sector to go to Texas, Maffit reasoned that he now had an opportunity to reverse his earlier trip and escape to the Gulf. On the night of January 15 he succeeded, speeding between two

John Newland Maffit: born at sea in 1819, the son of a Methodist minister, he attended school in Fayetteville, North Carolina; became a midshipman in the U.S. Navy in 1832; passed midshipman in 1837; married Mary Florence Murrell, who died in 1852; that same year he married Mrs. Caroline Laurens Read, and after she died, Maffit married Emma Martin; he served on the frigate *Constitution* in 1835, and then worked sixteen years on the U.S. Coastal Survey, charting the Atlantic Coast; promoted to lieutenant in 1843, he commanded first the brig *Dolphin*, which stopped slave ships and captured the *Echo*, and then commanded the *Crusader*, performing similar tasks; Maffit resigned his command in April 1861; he entered the Confederate naval service as a lieutenant, participating in action at Hilton Head, South Carolina, and mapping roads and obstructing the Coosaw River for Robert E. Lee; promoted to captain in 1862, Maffit commanded the *Cecile*, running the blockade to bring in arms and ammunition; early in 1863, he commanded the *Florida*, which he equipped and sent to Mobile; from September 1863 to June 1864 he commanded the *Florie* and the *Lucile*, destroying more than $10 million in Union property; Maffit took command of the ironclad *Albemarle* in the fall of 1864; denounced as a pirate by the Federals, he never surrendered; in March 1865, when the Confederate cause seemed

lost, he became a captain in the British navy; returning to the United States two years later, he settled on a farm and wrote his memoirs, *The Nautilus* (1878), and a sketch of Raphael Semmes for the *South Atlantic Magazine* (1877). Maffit died in Wilmington, North Carolina, in 1877.

C.S.S. *Florida*

powerful warships to reach the Gulf of Mexico and commence a cruise that would ultimately claim twenty Union merchantmen by August.

Back in Texas waters, the U.S. Navy seemed unable to regain its balance. With three major vessels lost, discipline and security tightened aboard the Union vessels as Commodore Bell sought some way to reestablish the tight blockade of the coast. Besides the squadron off Galveston, Captain John Dillingham commanded the U.S.S. *Morning Light*, an eight-gun former clipper ship, and the sailing schooner *Velocity*, off Sabine Pass.

Magruder wanted those ships. The same tactics employed at Galveston, he reasoned, would certainly work at Sabine Pass. Workers under the command of Major Smith fitted the *Josiah H. Bell*, a fairly large side-wheel steamer, with an eight-inch Columbiad rebored as a rifle in its bow. Stacked cotton bales formed a parapet for riflemen. Gunners of Company F, 1st Texas Heavy Artillery, filed on board to crew the cannon while Captain Charles Fowler made his way to the pilot house. The ship's consort, the *Uncle Ben*, was smaller, with cotton armor on deck and two 12-pounders poking from its bow. Captain K.D. Keith led his company over the gangplank to serve these pieces. Riflemen from Spaight's Battalion and the 2d Texas Cavalry manned the cotton-bale walls on both vessels. Magruder dispatched Major Oscar M. Watkins of his staff to organize and command the expedition.

Watkins planned for the sortie to take place on January 18, but weather intervened. With the ships loaded and the men anxious for a fight, a "norther" blew in that effectively shoved all of the water in Sabine Lake out to sea. Stranded, the two gunboats and their crews had to shiver in the wind until the weather changed. On January 20, the wind let up and Watkins ordered a foraging expedition sent to shoot some beeves on the prairie. Meanwhile, the commander of the expedition got drunk. As the tide lifted the boats off the bottom, Captain Fowler took the initiative to order the attack to proceed and the gunboats got up steam for Sabine Pass.

Taking advantage of a calm morning on January 21, 1863, Fowler and Johnson superceded their inebriated commander and ran their boats out to sea, knowing that the Union sailing vessels would lie becalmed. On board the *Morning Light* Captain Dillingham, seeing the Texans heading out, ordered all available sail made and signaled to the *Velocity* to get under way. Slowly the creaking vessels responded, but the Rebel steamers rapidly gained ground.

The stern chase lasted for several hours as the Union blockaders ran for deeper water. For thirty miles the *Josiah H. Bell* and *Uncle Ben* pursued. When Fowler's vessel had closed to within two miles, its rifled cannon opened upon the *Morning Light*. Captain Frederick Odlum and Lieutenant Richard Dowling served the piece, sending their first shot bounding off the main mast, and the second through a ship's boat. The third round stuck in the tube. Instead of abandoning the gun, Odlum and Dowling used sheer brute force to seat the shell and their fire continued. The next two shots splintered the *Morning Light's* deck and tangled its mainmast rigging. With rounds spinning through his lines and careening off of his deck, Dillingham sought to turn his vessel and bring his four broadside 32-pounders to bear. The nimble Confederates, however, kept out of the way.

When the ships closed to within rifle range, the Union vessels were doomed. Enfield bullets cleared the deck of the *Morning Light*, hitting thirteen men. His guns now untenable, and with the Texans knocking holes in his ship, Dillingham ordered his magazines flooded and struck his colors. The *Velocity*, soon overtaken by the *Uncle Ben*, also surrendered. Some 109 Union sailors now faced captivity as jubilant Texans clambered aboard the two ships.

Their time of celebration, though, would have to be short if the Texans would make good their conquests. Watkins ordered a prize crew put aboard both captured vessels, then ordered that all available speed be made back for Sabine Pass. The two steamers and the shallow-draft *Velocity* reached Sabine Lake without incident. The *Morning Light*, however, stuck fast on the bar. The Confederates set the ship afire to prevent it being recaptured.

The entire Confederate nation gloried in the exploits of the Texas cottonclads. The Congress passed a unanimous resolution of thanks to Magruder and his men. The names of the commanders were common knowledge in the halls of the Confederate capital. Magruder, extremely proud of his men, crowed to Governor Francis R. Lubbock, writing, "It gives me great pleasure to be able to announce to you, as I now do, that the coast of Texas is…free for the occupation of our troops from Sabine to the Rio Grande; that the enemy no longer has a foothold on the soil of Texas, and that his blockading squadron are his best ships, which keep a respectful distance from our shores."

Magruder's acting assistant adjutant general Stephen D. Yancey, waxed more eloquent. "The whole country has been electrified by the daring and skill of Texans, while the hearts of their comrades battling in the north for their homes and altars have been made to beat with pride and joy by the news of battles fought and victories won on the beloved soil of their glorious state." Yancey continued, trumpeting that "the commanding general of the Army of Texas is confident that his troops will…astonish still more their enemies and the world by such evidences of skill and audacity as shall make the word 'Texan' a better word than 'Spartan.'"

The efforts of these Texans, so it seemed, served mainly as a much needed morale boost for the Confederacy's flagging spirits. The exploits of Magruder's cottonclads, as well as the *Alabama* and *Florida*, launched 1863 with stirring news. But by midsummer, Southern fortunes seemed reversed with double disasters at Gettysburg and Vicksburg. Again, stout-hearted Texans serving their guns along the Gulf of Mexico delivered to the Confederate nation a little good news to ease its suffering.

9

THE BATTLE OF SABINE PASS

Spartans or not, Magruder had decided after his run of luck in January to strengthen his line of defenses. Most available guns and troops would concentrate in the Eastern Sub-District of Texas between Sabine Pass and Velasco. Engineer Colonel Valery Sulakowski, a Pole, and German Major Getulius Kellersberger designed a new series of fortifications that would protect the Lone Star coast. The Western Sub-District of Texas—Brazos Santiago, Corpus Christi, and Matagorda Bay— would be held, but only lightly.

The defenses of Galveston would receive priority. Sulakowski designed a series of works that not only fronted the Gulf but ringed the harbor with firepower. A gang of 2,000 slaves provided the labor, laying railroad spurs to batteries, building earthworks, and emplacing both real and "Quaker" guns. Engineers constructed railway rams that could move into position, fire, then withdraw before being discovered. All told, by year's end nearly a dozen new forts and redoubts sprang up housing some thirty-one cannon.

To the east, Texans reoccupied Sabine Pass. Also using slave labor, Texans constructed Fort Griffin in May 1863. Lieutenant Nicholas H. Smith, assigned to oversee completion of the post, described his position in unfavorable terms. His men needed equipment, he argued, as "some of the men are naked and others barefooted. All want something." In addition, pests made the climate intolerable. "The musquetoes are so bad here that it is almost impossible for a man or horse to live." He shared advice for other troops coming to that post. "Should it ever be your misfortune to be sent to this accursed all places, bring with you a [mosquito] bar sufficiently large for you to lay with your feet stratched out, for I am just out of bed and my feet are so badly swollen than I can hardly wear a shoe." He also complained that writing reports and letters exposed portions of his body to severe suffering. "My hands are blistered writing this letter. Allow for the imagination."

In another letter, marked as having been posted from "Headquarters, Army [of] Musquetoes," Smith reported on the progress of the fort. "I am here...for God knows how long," he wrote. Faced with increasing pressure to get the work built, Smith began to buckle under the strain of demanding sched-ules and inadequate materiel. "You know what it is to finish up a piece of work like this and have no material to do it with." His list of tasks left to complete seemed staggering. "I have the quarters of the troops to build yet, some where near one thousand feet of piling to drive, the fort to palisade, four Guns yet to Mount with God Knows how much more. To commence with I have not one pile, about fifty palisades, no lumber for quarters.... Oh curse the luck. I wish I was back in Galveston."

His companions in misery included Captain Frederick H. Odlum's Company F, 1st Texas Heavy Artillery. Veteran troops, these gunners had participated in the capture of U.S. forces at the time of secession, and had fought during the fall and recapture of Galveston as well as the capture of the *Morning Light*. Composed of Irish dockhands and laborers from Houston, the "Davis Guards" followed the lead of Odlum's brother-in-law, Lieutenant Richard Dowling, in Odlum's absence.

Dowling was a popular man with his troops. A native of County Galway, Ireland, he had immigrated to Texas in the mid-1850s. Described as "boyish" with rosy cheeks, blue eyes, and reddish brown hair, he had a reputation for cheerfulness. An entrepreneur, Dowling owned a succession of extremely successful saloons and billiard halls described consistently as... "the best in the state." Dowling's forty-two gunners were experienced and well-drilled. While engineer officers fussed over completing Fort Griffin, the "Davis Guards" practiced at their guns, placing range markers in the channels of Sabine Pass.

Further south, earthworks appeared at all of the state's strategic points. At Velasco, troops constructed a strong work mounting six 32-pounders. Near Saluria, workers rebuilt and strengthened Fort Esparanza which mounted two 12-pounders, five 24-pounders, and a ten-inch Columbiad. Major Daniel Shea led 500 men to the Matagorda Island post to man these guns. The *Lucy Gwinn*, now armed and cottonclad, arrived to patrol the bay.

Union planners knew that Magruder was digging in, but they had faced more daunting tasks further east. After the capture of the Mississippi, Union leaders decided that an opportunity existed—with the availability of now unoccupied army and navy assets—to strike into Texas and occupy the upper coast once and for all. Accordingly, an overland expedition fitted out along Bayou Teche in Louisiana that would press against Richard Taylor's Confederate army there and plunge into eastern Texas. Meanwhile, an amphibious operation would drive into Sabine Pass, land troops, cut the railroad from Houston to Beaumont, and prevent Magruder from sending reinforcements to aid Taylor. By early Fall, the Federals reasoned, Union forces would physically occupy the Gulf Coast as far as Galveston Bay, and the Island City itself would be again untenable for the Rebels.

The initial invasion force was impressive. To accomplish the landings in Texas, Union authorities authorized General William B. Franklin to load three infantry brigades, ten batteries of artillery, and four companies of the 1st Texas Cavalry (Union) onto eighteen transports. Escorting this fleet were four gunboats under Lieutenant Frederick Crocker, himself a veteran of these waters. The warships included the Galveston veterans *Clifton* and *Sachem*, along with U.S.S. *Granite City*

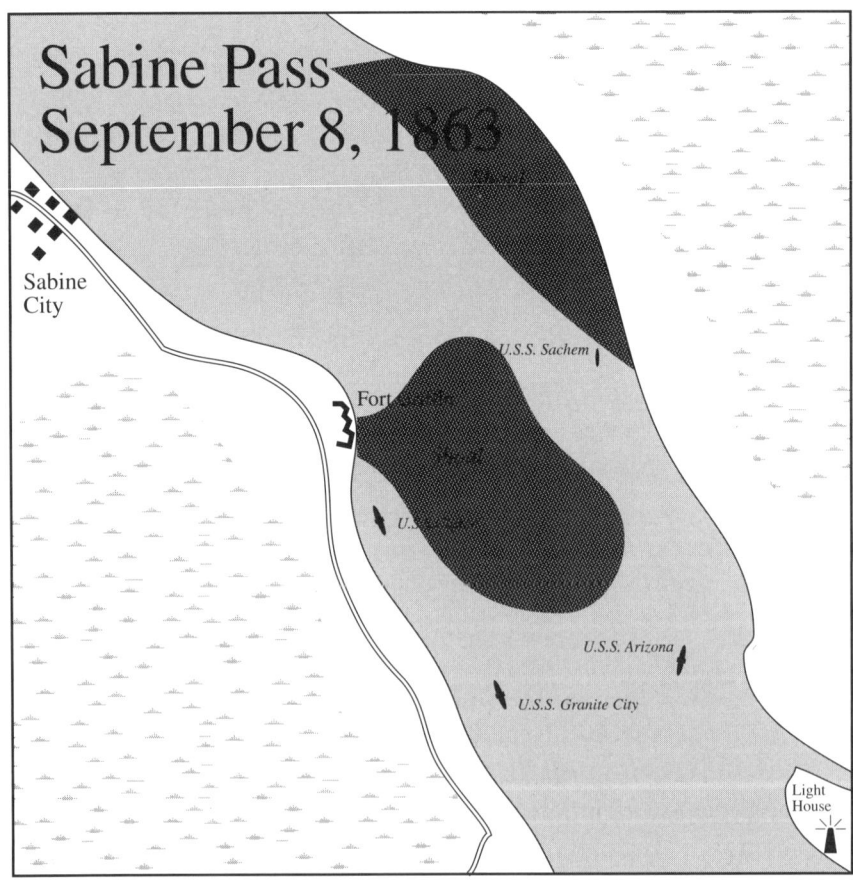

and U.S.S. *Arizona*. The gunboats would shell Fort Griffin while infantrymen would wade ashore and carry the work from its land side. All together, the U.S. Navy counted nearly twenty heavy cannon to pound the six Rebel guns into submission.

Despite these odds, Union plans went awry. Crocker sent *Granite City* ahead to mark the channel over the bar. When that vessel arrived on station, its commander spied a silhouette on the horizon out to sea. Fearing that this unknown ship was the C.S.S. *Alabama*, and mindful of the fate of the *Hatteras* earlier in the year, the Union officer ordered his vessel to flee. Meanwhile, the rest of Crocker's flotilla arrived to find *Granite City* missing, and spent precious time searching for their missing consort. At the same time, the troop transports arrived as scheduled and crossed the bar unescorted, almost blundering into the Rebel guns before discovering their mistake. Sheepishly the Federals retired, having given the Texans at Fort Griffin a good preview of the forces at hand.

Even with the advanced warning, Texans at Sabine Pass doubted their ability to hold their position. On the night of September 7, 1863, Dowling nervously prepared for battle. His men scurried to their two 24-pounders and their four 32-pounders while couriers sped north to hurry forward reinforcements. The next morning, C.S.S. *Uncle Ben* cast off from its moorings in Sabine Lake. "Lieut. Harris and half our men were ordered aboard Gun Boat to act as borders in case any of the boats got past the fort," wrote one Texan. At the same time, he and the other Rebel cavalrymen stood near the fort. "I had the balance of our men and horses in rear of the fort to run or fight as the case might happen." Meanwhile Major Leon Smith at Beaumont directed troops to load onto the small steamer *Roebuck*. At the opposite end of the lake, the C.S.S. *Josiah H. Bell* and the tender *Florilda* took on men and started toward the Pass. Dowling was determined to keep the Federals out of Sabine Lake, but failing that, he hoped that the cottonclads nearby might retrieve the situation.

Crocker began the action on the morning of September 8, 1863, by commanding his flagship U.S.S. *Clifton* to steam over the bar and probe the enemy defenses. That vessel complied and fired twenty-six rifled shells at the position before retiring. Having received no return fire, the Union officer surmised that they were facing smoothbores alone. Based on that information, Crocker ordered three of his gunboats to the attack while the transports and the remaining combatant followed to effect the landings. To aid in the assault, crews aboard the warships loaned their ships' boats to the army to ferry men to shore.

On shore, the Davis Guards spent a nervous morning. Reinforcements dribbled in, including the fiery Leon Smith and assistant surgeon George H. Bailey who was on hand, according to Dowling, to "administer Magruder Pills to the enemy." The citizens of Sabine City slaughtered a beef for the gunners and provided sweet potatoes, biscuits, and coffee besides.

The attack began by mid-afternoon. The Union gunboats divided and started up the Pass at 3:30 P.M. The U.S.S. *Clifton* took the west, or Texas, channel while *Sachem* and *Arizona* took the east. Opening fire at extreme range, the Federal crews sent rifled rounds zipping toward the earthwork. One round smashed the elevating screw of one cannon while Dowling hunkered down in a corner of the fort and watched as the enemy drew near, his men huddled in bomb proofs awaiting his orders. As the Union vessels came closer, smoke from the Rebel cottonclads could be seen off in Sabine Lake.

As *Sachem*, leading the attack, drew opposite the fort, crewmen noticed pilings and stakes in the water, and soon learned that these were the target points that Dowling's gunners had been practicing on. Dowling yelled for his men, who boiled out of their hiding places, to man their guns. Immediately the Texans opened a rapid fire, firing two shots per gun to get the range, and then holing the *Sachem* several times. Without taking time to swab their guns, Dowling's Irishmen were managing a round a minute out of their heavy guns. As the *Sachem* submitted to this pounding, the crew heard the sickening sound of its hull crunching against mud and gravel as the vessel came to a halt.

As the horror of this event sank in, an even more dreadful disaster befell the ship. A Texan 24-pounder sent a shot careening through the boat and severed the steam pipe, a cloud of scalding steam erupting from the deck. The U.S.S. *Arizona*, by now receiving much of Fort Griffin's attention, reversed engines and backed away from the debacle. The *Sachem* struck its colors.

Conditions inside Fort Griffin were by no means comfortable. "The shot and shells tumbled into the fort...like apples falling from a heavily loaded tree," reported one Texan. As the fight intensified, one Rebel came forward with the company flag of one of the local cavalry commands. Dowling took the standard and, mounting the parapet, planted the colors defiantly. The rapid fire, though, had exhausted his men. One 24-pounder had tumbled off its platform in the barrage, and many men were burned from serving the guns. Some 137 rounds would fly from Dowling's guns in the course of the fight, and his forty-two men were beginning to fade from fatigue.

Meanwhile, U.S.S. *Clifton* planned to take advantage of the fort's confusion by dashing in close and killing the Texan crews with lethal broadsides of grapeshot. Gathering momentum, the large ferryboat was gaining its objective when one Rebel gun began to find its range. A chance shot struck the *Clifton's* tiller rope, sending the speeding ship out of control and into shoal water. Careening to one side, the ship lay helpless as the Texans pounded away at its hull. Within moments, *Clifton's* boiler exploded. Crocker surrendered his stricken ship.

Franklin watched in horror as the attack unraveled. Fearing that Union reports had underestimated the defenses at Sabine Pass, he called off the landing and ordered his transports back across the bar. Two of his ships grounded, forcing him to order scores of hobbled horses and mules and some

200,000 rations thrown overboard to lighten the load. Upon reaching the Gulf, the Federals withdrew to New Orleans, leaving behind 315 of their comrades as prisoners and nearly seventy killed, wounded, or missing.

Near Fort Griffin, Union sailors began leaping overboard to swim or wade to shore. Dowling, believing these troops to be a landing party, ordered his red hot guns loaded with grapeshot. Upon closer examination, he discovered that the men were surrendering.

The Texans could not believe their good fortune. "Had they passed the fort today, [they] would have been in Houston flanking Galveston causing us to evacuate the Island," wrote a Rebel defender. "All honor and praise is due this artillery company, the Davis Guards, for saving this section of the country for the present." For miles down the coast, crates of crackers and barrels of bacon littered the beach, as did bloated carcasses of drowned horses and mules.

Certain that the Federals would be back, Engineer Lieutenant Smith was in no mood to be chirpy about this amazing success. "This place is hell," he wrote as he fretted over completing the still unfinished Fort Griffin. Col [Sulakowski] is in more of a hurry that he was in Galveston. I am working now about 18 hours in 24." Before long, slaves and sappers mounted the cannon from the *Clifton* and *Sachem* behind extensive earthworks near Fort Griffin.

The results of this battle, like the events earlier in the year, were electrifying to the nation. The Confederate Congress again voted its thanks to the Texans. Special medals were stamped for Dowling's gunners. Stock prices fell in New York, and the Northern public had to temper its earlier ebullience. After the loss of seven warships in nine months, Texas had become a dangerous place for the U.S. Navy. The Anaconda, at least for that stretch of the Confederate coast, remained at bay.

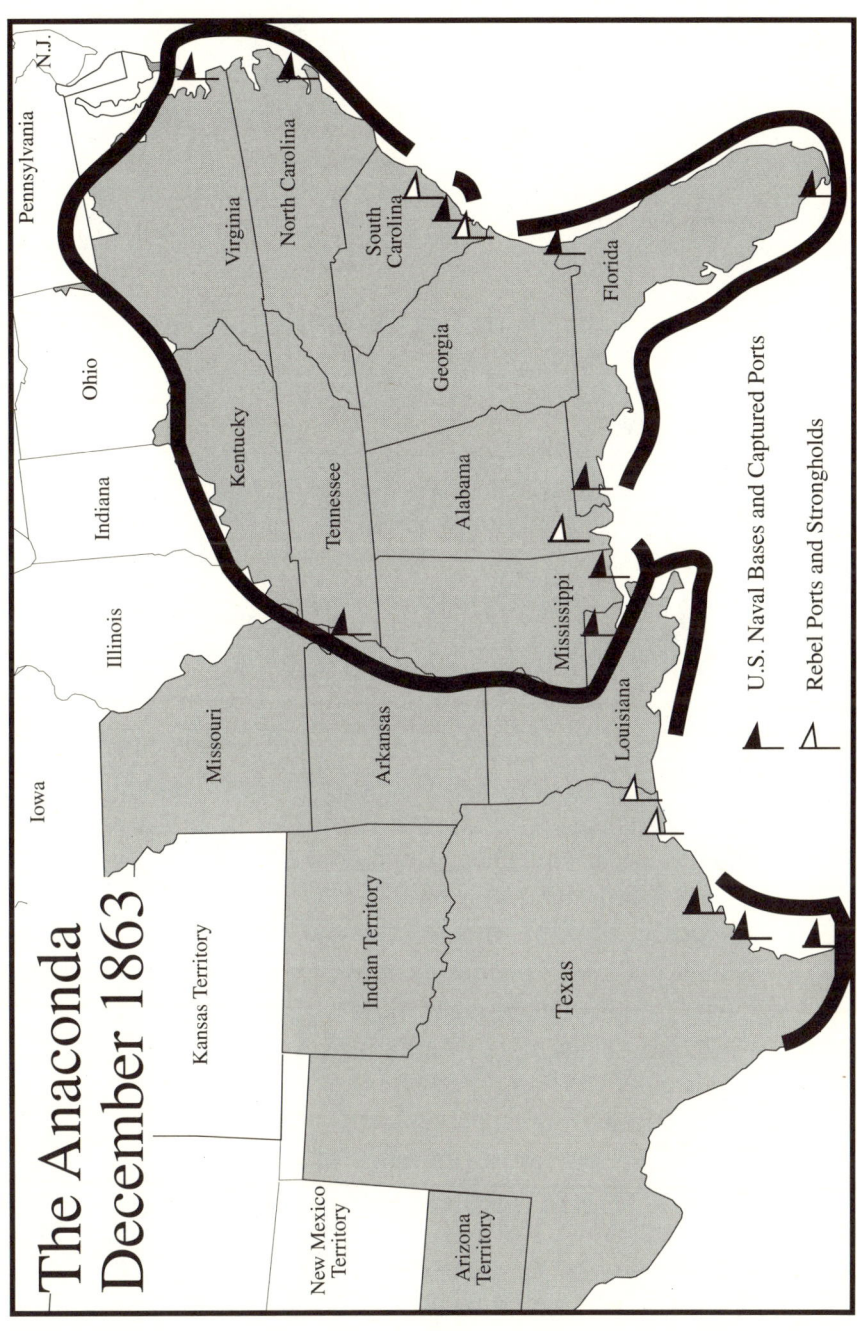

The Anaconda
December 1863

U.S. Naval Bases and Captured Ports

Rebel Ports and Strongholds

10
BLOCKADE RUNNERS ON THE TEXAS COAST

Despite the disasters in 1863, Union troops did finally achieve success on the lower Texas Coast. On November 2, 1863, General Nathaniel P. Banks led a 7,000-man expedition that captured Brazos Santiago and moved inland to take Brownsville. Two weeks later, his Federals landed on Mustang Island and captured the garrison and defenses of Corpus Christi. On November 21, Major General Cadwallader C. Washburn landed troops on Matagorda Island and forced the abandonment of Fort Esparanza. By the end of the year, Union troops occupied Indianola and had skirmished with Texans on the San Bernard River, but failed to move further inland. By early the next year, most of the Federals had left.

Banks's offensive would be the last Union threat to the Texas coast, and it soon became the Confederacy's leading haven for blockade runners. Daring captains carried thousands of bales of cotton to Gulf and Caribbean ports, and brought in a wide variety of cargoes, split almost evenly between military supplies and high-profit luxury items. The volume of this traffic continued until the end of the war, prompting the U.S. Navy to assign twenty ships to the blockade of Texas, quite a sizable increase from the half-dozen or so routinely on station. Even so, Texas could not overcome its geographic remoteness. The economic lifeblood of the Confederacy continued to be drained by the Union navy in other waters, which contributed to the nation's demise.

Galveston, the most important city in Texas, would not again witness the arrival of Union warships to its wharves until June 2, 1865. On that day, Confederate authorities surrendered the Army of the Trans-Mississippi aboard the U.S.S. *Fort Jackson.* This final act in the failure of Southern independence occurred in the Confederacy's last major unoccupied port.

APPENDIX A

ORGANIZATION OF CONFEDERATE FORCES

CONFEDERATE LAND FORCES ALONG TEXAS COAST, SEPTEMBER 20, 1863

Eastern Sub-District of Texas
COLONEL PHILIP NOLAN LUCKETT

GALVESTON (COL. X. B. DEBRAY)
1st Cavalry Battalion, Arizona Brigade (Davidson's)
26th Texas Cavalry (DeBray's)
20th Texas Infantry (Elmore's)
1st Texas Heavy Artillery (Cook's)
Mosely's Texas Field Artillery Battery
(formerly Co. D, 13th Texas Infantry)
14th Texas Field Artillery Battery (Dashiell's)
Howe's Heavy Artillery Battery (Engineers)

SABINE PASS (COL. A. BUCHEL)
1st Texas Heavy Artillery (Companies A and F)
12th Texas Cavalry Battalion (Brown's)
(later combined with Rountree's Texas Cavalry Battalion to form 35th Texas Cavalry)
1st Texas Cavalry (Buchel's)
(composed of 3rd Texas Cavalry Battalion and 8th Texas Cavalry Battalion)
23rd Texas Cavalry (Gould's)
21st Texas Infantry Battalion (Griffin's)
(later combined with Spaight's 11th Texas Infantry Battalion to form 21st Texas Infantry Regiment)
3rd Texas Infantry (Luckett's)
Jones's Texas Field Artillery Battery
(later combined with Mosely's Battery to form 7th Texas Artillery Battalion)

LIBERTY
36th Texas Cavalry (Woods's)

VELASCO

13th Texas Infantry (Bates's)

(serving in Louisiana during summer of 1863)

Western Sub-District of Texas
BRIG. GEN. HAMILTON P. BEE

RIO GRANDE TO CORPUS CHRISTI

33rd Texas Cavalry (Duff's)

Willke's Field Artillery Battalion (Four Companies)

8th Infantry Battalion (Hobby's), part

(later combined with 4th Texas Artillery Battalion to form 8th Texas Infantry Regiment)

MATAGORDA BAY

4th Texas Artillery Battalion (Shea's)

   Vernon's Battery

   Reuss's Battery

8th Infantry Battalion (Hobby's), part

(later combined with 4th Texas Artillery Battalion to form 8th Texas Infantry Regiment)

OTHER TROOPS THAT PERIODICALLY SERVED ON THE TEXAS COAST

2d Texas Infantry, 1864–1865

(composed of soldiers exchanged after fall of Vicksburg)

Waul's Texas Legion, 1864–1865

(composed of soldiers exchanged after fall of Vicksburg)

11th Texas Infantry Battalion (Spaight's)

(serving in Louisiana during summer of 1863)

2d Texas Cavalry (Pyron's)

(serving in Louisiana during summer of 1863)

4th Texas Cavalry (Reily's)

(December 1862–March 1863; December 1863–March 1864)

5th Texas Cavalry (Green's)

(December 1862–March 1863; December 1863–March 1864)

7th Texas Cavalry (Bagby's)

(December 1862–March 1863; December 1863–March 1864)

35th Texas Cavalry (Likens's)

(composed of Likens's Texas Cavalry Battalion and Burns's Texas Cavalry Battalion)

37th Texas Cavalry (Terrell's)
8th Texas Field Artillery Battery (Fox's)
13th Texas Field Artillery Battery (Gonzales')
(serving in Louisiana during summer of 1863)
15th Texas Field Artillery Battery (Nichols')
(serving in Louisiana during summer of 1863)
16th Texas Field Artillery Battery (Gibson's)

APPENDIX B

ORGANIZATION OF UNION FORCES

UNION LAND FORCES

BATTLE OF GALVESTON, JANUARY 1863
1st Texas Cavalry (Union)
42nd Massachusetts Infantry (Companies D, G, I)
2nd Vermont Battery

SABINE PASS EXPEDITION, SEPTEMBER 1863
XIX ARMY CORPS (MAJ. GEN. WILLIAM B. FRANKLIN)
FIRST DIVISION (BRIG. GEN. GODFREY WEITZEL)

1st Brigade (Col. George M. Love)
30th MA.
116th NY
161st NY
174th NY

3rd Brigade (Col. Robert Merritt)
12th CT
75th NY
114th NY
160th NY
8th VT

1st Brigade, Third Division (Brig. Gen. Frank Nickerson)
110th NY
162nd NY
165th NY
14th ME

Artillery
A, 1st U.S.
F, 1st U.S.
L, 1st U.S.
1st Indiana Heavy Artillery
2nd MA Battery
4th MA Battery
6th MA Battery
1st VT Battery
1st ME Battery
18th NY Battery

BANKS'S TEXAS COAST OPERATIONS, NOVEMBER-DECEMBER 1863
XIII ARMY CORPS (MAJ. GEN. NAPOLEON J.T. DANA)

WASHBURN'S COMMAND (Maj. Gen. Cadwallader C. Washburn)

HEADQUARTERS AT MATAGORDA BAY, TEXAS
FIRST DIVISION (BRIG. GEN. WILLIAM P. BENTON)
1st Brigade (Brig. Gen. Fitz Henry Warren)
33rd IL
99th IL
8th IN
18th IN

2nd Brigade (Col. Charles L. Harris)
21st IA
22nd IA
23rd IA
11th WI

3rd Brigade (Col. James Keigwin)
69th IN
16th OH
114th OH

3rd Brigade, Second Division (Brig. Gen. Thomas E.G. Ransom)
34th IA
13th ME
15th ME

FOURTH DIVISION (COL. WILLIAM J. LANDRAM)

1st Brigade (Lt. Col. John Cowan)
60th IN
67th IN
19th KY
83rd OH
96th OH
23rd WI

2nd Brigade (Maj. Memoir V. Hotchkiss)
77th IL
130th IL
48th OH

Artillery
Chicago Mercantile Battery
17th OH Battery
7th MI Battery
F, 1st MO

Independent Organizations
19th Infantry, Corps d'Afrique
1st Indiana Heavy Artillery

DANA'S COMMAND (MAJ. GEN. NAPOLEON J. T. DANA)

HEADQUARTERS AT BROWNSVILLE, TEXAS
SECOND DIVISION (MAJ. GEN. NAPOLEON J. T. DANA)

1st Brigade (Col. J. Charles Black)
37th IL
91st IL
26th IN
38th IA

2nd Brigade (Col. William McE. Dye)

94th IL

19th IA

20th IA

20th WI

Artillery

B, 1st MO

E, 1st MO

Independent Organizations

1st Texas Cavalry (Union)

2nd Texas Cavalry (Union)

Vidal's Company Partisan Rangers

Pioneer Company

Provost Guard Company

1st Engineers, Corps d'Afrique

2nd Engineers, Corps d'Afrique

16th Infantry, Corps d'Afrique

APPENDIX C

CONFEDERATE AND UNITED STATES SHIPS

All ship information taken from

Silverstone, Paul H. *Warships of the Civil War Navies.*
Annapolis: United States Naval Institute Press, 1989.

CONFEDERATE WARSHIPS MENTIONED

C.S.S. *Alabama*
Bark-rigged, sloop of war, single funnel, wooden hull
(launched May 15, 1862, commissioned August 24, 1862)

Dimensions: 1,050 tons, 220' length, 31' 9" beam.
Speed: 13 knots
Crew: 148
Armament: 6x 32pd SB; 1x 110pd R, 1 eight-inch SB

War record: Commissioned at sea off of the Azores Islands, this English built
cruiser took more than sixty Union prizes and destroyed the U.S.S.
Hatteras off of Galveston on January 11, 1863. Destroyed by U.S.S.
Kearsarge off Cherbourg, June 19, 1864.

C.S.S. *Bayou City*
Side-wheel wooden river steamboat
(launched August 1859, commissioned February 1862)

Dimensions: 165' length, 28' beam, 5' draft.
Speed: 7 knots?
Crew: 135
Armament: 1x 32pdSB converted to Rifle

War record: Built in Jeffersonville, Indiana. Serving as mechant steamer in
Galveston Bay at beginning of the war, the *Bayou City* participated in
the ramming and capture of the U.S.S. *Harriet Lane* on January 1,
1863. The vessel served the rest of the war in Galveston Bay.

C.S.S. *Florida*
Sloop-rigged, two funnels, iron hull.
(launched January 1862, commissioned August 17, 1862)

Dimensions: 700 tons. 191' length, 27' 3" beam.
Speed: 9.5 knots; 12 knots under sail
Crew: 52

Armament: 6x 6" R; 2x 110pd R, 1 12pd How

War record: Commissioned at Green Cay, Bahamas Islands, this English built cruiser had been designed as an iron-hulled gunboat for the Italian navy. As C.S.S. *Florida* it took more than thirty Union prizes. Captured by U.S.S. *Wachusett* off Bahia, Brazil, October 7, 1864. Sank in collision with transport *Alliance* off Newport News, Virginia, November 28, 1864.

Steamer Florilda
Side-wheel wooden river steamboat
(launched 1857)

Dimensions: 304 tons

War record: This Louisville, Kentucky built steamboat served as a railroad utility vessel in Beaumont before the war. During the war, the vessel served as a troop transport in Sabine Lake.

C.S.S. *John F. Carr*
Side-wheel wooden river steamboat

War record: Small vessel serving as a mechant steamer in Galveston Bay at beginning of the war, the *John F. Carr* participated in the capture of the U.S.S. *Harriet Lane* on January 1, 1863. The vessel served the rest of the war in Matagorda Bay where it was wrecked in early 1864.

C.S.S. *Josiah H. Bell*
Side-wheel wooden river steamboat
(launched 1853, commissioned February 1862)

Dimensions: 412 tons, 171' length, 30' beam, 6.7' draft.
Speed: 7 knots?
Crew: 150
Armament: 1x eight-inch Columbiad

War record: Built in Jeffersonville, Indiana. This large riverboat was serving as the merchant steamer *J.H. Bell* in Sabine Lake at beginning of the war. The *Josiah H. Bell* participated in the capture of the U.S.S. *Morning Light* on January 20, 1863. The vessel served the rest of the war in Sabine Lake, where it was scuttled in 1865.

C.S.S. *Lucy Gwinn*
Stern-wheel wooden river steamboat
(Launched 1859, commissioned February 1862)

Dimensions: 152 tons

War record: Built in Freedom, Pennsylvania. This small vessel served as a merchant steamer along the Texas coast at beginning of the war. The *Lucy Gwinn* participated in the capture of the U.S.S. *Harriet Lane* on January 1, 1863. The vessel served the rest of the war in Matagorda Bay where it was surrendered at the end of the war. The ship evidently never fell into Union hands as it was reported removed to Matamoros, Tamaulipas, Mexico.

C.S.S. *Neptune*
Side-wheel wooden steam tugboat

Crew: 100
Armament: 2x 24pd How

War record: This small ship was serving as U.S. Mail packet in Galveston Bay at beginning of the war. The *Neptune* participated in the ramming and capture of the U.S.S. *Harriet Lane* on January 1, 1863. Sunk by cannon fire from U.S.S. *Harriet Lane* and U.S.S. *Owasco*, the *Neptune* sank in shallow water but was never repaired.

Steamer Roebuck
Side-wheel wooden river steamboat
(launched 1857)

Dimensions: 164 tons, 147' length, 23' beam, 5' draft.

War record: This steamboat, built on the Ohio River, served as a merchant steamer in Sabine Lake at beginning of the war. The vessel served as a troop transport in Sabine Lake during the war.

C.S.S. *Uncle Ben*
Side-wheel wooden river steamboat

Dimensions: 135 tons
Armament: 2x 12pd How

War record: Small ship serving as merchant steamer in Sabine Lake at beginning of the war. The *Uncle Ben* participated in the capture of the U.S.S. *Velocity* on January 20, 1863. The vessel served the rest of the war in Sabine Lake.

UNITED STATES WARSHIPS MENTIONED

U.S.S. *Arizona*
Large side-wheel combatant, iron-hulled two masted schooner
(launched 1859, acquired January 23, 1863)

Dimensions: 950 tons, 201' 6" length, 34' beam, 10' draft.
Crew: 91
Armament (Jan 1863): 4x 32pd; 1x 30pd R; 1x 12pd R

War record: Started war as blockade runner *Caroline* until captured by U.S.S. *Montgomery* off Pensacola on October 29, 1862. Transferred to Louisiana where it engaged C.S.S. *Queen of the West* in Grand Lake on April 14, 1863, and captured Fort Burton on April 20. Served in Red River in May 1863, then participated in attack on Sabine Pass, September 8. Served the rest of the war blockading Texas coast until destroyed by fire in the Mississippi River on February 27, 1865. Took one prize.

U.S.S. *Brooklyn*
Screw sloop, ship rigged.
(launched July 27, 1858, commissioned January 26, 1859)

Dimensions: 2,532 tons, 233' length, 43' beam, 16' 3" draft.
Speed: 11.5 knots
Crew: 335
Armament (Jan 1863): 24x IX-inch Dahlgren; 2x 12pd How

War record: Involved in passage of forts Jackson and St. Philip and combat with CSN vessels, April 24, 1862; bombardment of Grand Gulf, Mississippi, May 26, 1862; passage of Vicksburg batteries, June 28, 1862; attack on Vicksburg July 22, 1862. On station at Pensacola and Mobile, then ordered to Galveston, January 1863, before ordered laid up for repairs August 1863–April 1864. Severely damaged, Battle of Mobile Bay, August 5, and bombardment of Fort Morgan, August 9–23, 1864. Transferred to Atlantic where it served in the attack on Fort Fisher, North Carolina, December 24–25, 1864 and January 13–15 1865. Served off South America 1865–1867 and Europe 1871–1873. Served in the North and South Atlantic in 1874–1875 before being trimmed down and rebuilt, 1876–1881. Returned to coast of South America where *Brooklyn* suffered a collision with British steamer *Mozart* at Montevideo on May 1, 1882. Repaired and ordered to China, 1886–1889. Decommissioned May 14, 1889 and sold for scrap March 25, 1891.

U.S.S. *Cayuga*
Screw gunboat, two mast schooner rigged.
(launched October 21, 1861, commissioned February 21, 1862)

Dimensions: 691 tons, 158' 4" length, 28' beam, 9' 6" draft.
Speed: 10 knots
Crew: 114
Armament (Jan 1863): 1x XI-inch Dahlgren; 4x 24pd SB; 1x 20pd Parrot R

War record: Belonged to a class of vessels known popularly as "Ninety-Day Gunboats" because they were built quickly of unseasoned wood. Ordered as a stop-gap measure by the U.S. Navy, these ships sailed well but rolled heavily. Involved in passage of forts Jackson and St. Philip and combat with CSN vessels, April 24, 1862; bombardment of Baton Rouge and engagement with C.S.S. *Arkansas*, August 5, 1862; Occupation of Baton Rouge, December 17, 1862. Ordered to Texas January 1863. Patrolled Gulf Coast until end of war. Decommissioned July 31, 1865, sold October 25, 1865. Sailed as bark-rigged merchant ship *Veteran* until at least 1885. Captured six prizes.

U.S.S. *Clifton*
Ex-Ferryboats-4th Rate Side-wheel combatant.
(launched 1861, commissioned December 2, 1861)

Dimensions: 892 tons, 210' length, 40' beam, 13' 4" draft.
Crew: 121
Armament (Jan 1863): 2x IX-inch Dahlgren; 4x 32pd SB; 2x 30pd Parrot R

War record: New York Harbor ferryboats made excellent gunboats because of their agile maneuverability and their strengthened decks were capable of carrying heavy guns. U.S.S. *Clifton* participated in the passage of forts Jackson and St. Philip and the fight with the CSN vessels on April 24, 1862. Later, it fought at Vicksburg on June 26–28 where it was severely damaged by plunging fire from the bluffs. *Clifton* next went to Texas where it participated in the capture of Galveston on October 4, 1862 and the bombardment of Port Lavaca on October 31–November 1, 1862. After the disaster at Galveston on January 1, 1863, the vessel served in the Bayou Teche, Louisiana, campaign of April, 1863 where it helped disable the C.S.S. *Diana* and reduced Fort Burton at Butte-la-Rose on the Atchafalaya River. On September 8, U.S.S. *Clifton* fell prey to Rebel gunners at Sabine Pass, Texas where it struck its colors. Serving from that point on as a blockade runner, the C.S.S. *Clifton* struck a sandbar on March 21, 1864 in Sabine Pass and was burned to prevent its recapture by the U.S. Navy. This vessel took one prize.

U.S.S. *Corypheus*
Small Schooner
(launched 1851, acquired May 19, 1862)

Dimensions: 82 tons
Crew: 16
Armament (Jan 1863): 1x 24pd How; 1x 30pd Parrot R

War record: Small blockade runner captured by U.S.S. *Calhoun* in southeastern Louisiana on May 13, 1862. Served off of Louisiana and Texas coast before participating in Battle of Galveston on January 1, 1863. Continued with the West Gulf Blockading Squadron until war's end, when it was sold on September 15, 1865. Captured one prize.

U.S.S. Granite City
Medium side-wheel combatant-4th rate, two mast brigantine rigged.
(launched November 11, 1862, commissioned April 16, 1863)

Dimensions: 315 tons, 160' length, 23' beam, 9' 2" draft.
Crew: 69
Armament (1863): 1x 12pd R; 6x 24pd How

War record: Was blockade runner *Granite City*, captured by U.S.S. *Tioga* in the Bahama Islands, March 22, 1863. Involved in attack on Sabine Pass, September 8, 1863. Served along Texas coast until early 1864. Captured by Confederates at Calcasieu Pass, Louisiana, April 28, 1864. Took four prizes.

U.S.S. *Harriet Lane*
Medium side-wheel combatant-4th rate, two mast brigantine rigged.
(launched November 20, 1857, acquired September 17, 1861)

Dimensions: 750 tons, 180' length, 30' beam, 12' 6" draft.
Speed: 12 knots
Crew: 100
Armament (Jan 1863): 3x IX-inch Dahlgren; 1x 30pd Parrot R, 1x 12pd R

War record: Served as only steam powered vessel in the Revenue Service prior to the war. Served with the U.S. Navy in the Paraguay Expedition, 1858–1859. Tried to relieve Fort Sumter, South Carolina, April 12, 1861. Participated in the capture of Hatteras Inlet, August 28–29, and bombardment of Freestone Point, Virginia, December 9, 1861. Assigned to escort mortar flotilla to Mississippi River where it participated in the bombardment of forts Jackson and St. Philip April 18–28, 1862. Passed the forts and engaged CSN vessels on April 24, 1862. Steamed to Pensacola to cover Union occupation of harbor forts, then returned to participate in the operations against Vicksburg in June and July. Active in the capture of Galveston, October 4, 1862.

Captured by Confederates on January 1, 1863. Under the Confederates, *Harriet Lane* never again saw action as a warship, its guns removed to fortifications on the Red River. As blockade runner *Lavinia* made successful passage to Havana where it remained until war's end. Sold as bark-rigged merchant *Elliot Richie* and sailed as such until foundering in a storm off Pernambuco, Brazil, May 13, 1884. Captured five prizes.

U.S.S. *Hatteras*
Large Side-Wheel Combatant, 2nd Rate, Schooner rigged
(launched 1861, acquired September 25, 1861)

Dimensions: 1,126 tons, 210' length, 34' beam, 18' draft.
Crew: 110
Armament (Jan 1863): 4x 32pd SB; 1x 20pd Parrot R

War record: This iron hulled, three masted schooner was launched as the merchant *St. Mary's* but acquired quickly by the U.S. Navy. Led successful raid on Cedar Keys, Florida, January 16, 1862; engaged C.S.S. *Mobile* in Atchafalaya Bay, Louisiana, January 26, 1862. Patrolled Gulf Coast until ordered to Texas in January, 1863. Destroyed in action with C.S.S. *Alabama* off Galveston on January 11, 1863. Captured or destroyed more than fifteen enemy vessels.

U.S.S. *Henry Janes*
Two mast sailing vessel, schooner rigged.
(launched 1854, acquired September 27, 1861)

Dimensions: 261 tons, 109' 9" length, 29' 8" beam, 9' draft.
Crew: 35
Armament (Sept. 1862): 1x thirteen-inch Mortar; 2x 32pd SB

War record: Belonged to a class of vessels known as mortar schooners, converted merchant vessels to serve in the role of bombardment ships similar to the bomb ketches and brigs of the Mexican War. Grouped together into the Mississippi mortar flotilla, the *Henry Janes* and its consorts were instrumental in reducing forts Jackson and St. Philip, April 18–28, 1862. These ships bombarded Vicksburg from June 26 to July 22, with only a brief scare from C.S.S. *Arkansas*. The *Henry Janes* sailed to Texas in September, 1862, to aid in the reduction of Confederate defenses at Sabine Pass and Galveston. Returned to the Mississippi in time to serve in the siege of Port Hudson, May 8–July 9, 1863. Also served in Mobile Bay in February 1864 before having its mortar removed; ordered to the coast of Virginia. Decommissioned on July 12, 1865, and sold July 20, 1865. Accounted for two prizes.

U.S.S. *Kensington*
Screw auxiliary gunboat.
(launched 1858, acquired January 27, 1862)

Dimensions: 1,052 tons, 195' length, 31' 10" beam, 18' draft.
Crew: 72
Armament (Sept. 1862): 2x 32pd SB; 1x 30pd Parrot R

War record: This large, sluggish, wooden merchant ship served a peacetime commercial route from Philadelphia to Boston before being purchased as
a fleet tender by the U.S. Navy. Used mostly to supply food and water
to blockaders on station, U.S.S. *Kensington* did occasionally serve in
combat, aiding but not participating in the attack on Sabine Pass in
September, 1862. The vessel captured nine enemy ships in its career
before being decommissioned in May 1865 and sold as the merchant
Kensington in July of that year. Sank off of the Carolina coast on
January 27, 1871, after colliding with the Argentine bark *Templar*.

U.S.S. *Morning Light*
Clipper Ship
(launched August 15, 1853, acquired September 2, 1861)

Dimensions: 937 tons, 172' length, 34' 3" beam, 19' draft.
Crew: 120
Armament (Jan 1863): 8x 32pd SB

War record: Privately owned merchant ship bought by the navy. Patrolled Gulf
coast before ordered to station at Sabine Pass. Captured and burned
there on January 23, 1863. Took two prizes.

U.S.S. *New London*
Small screw combatant, three masted schooner rigged
(launched October 5, 1859, acquired August 26, 1861)

Dimensions: 221 tons, 135' length, 26' beam, 7' 8" draft.
Speed: 9.5 knots
Crew: 47
Armament (Jan 1863): 3x 32pd SB, 1x 42pd R, 1x 20pd Parrot R

War record: This wooden hulled screw schooner served its entire military career in
the Gulf and Mississippi, firing its first shots near Pass Christian,
Mississippi in March and April 1862. In Early 1863, *New London*
served on the coast of Texas before returning to the Mississippi where
it dueled Rebel field batteries near Donaldsonville. Disabled and partially destroyed on July 10, 1863. After repairs, continued to prowl
the Gulf Coast. Took thirteen prizes before being decommissioned in
August, 1865. Sold the next month, the ship sailed as the merchant
Acushnet until 1910.

U.S.S. *Owasco*
Screw gunboat, two mast schooner rigged.
(launched October 5, 1861, commissioned January 23, 1862)

Dimensions: 691 tons, 158' 4" length, 28' beam, 9' 6" draft.
Speed: 10 knots
Crew: 114
Armament (Jan 1863): 1x XI-inch Dahlgren; 2x 24pd SB; 1x 20pd Parrot R

War record: Belonged to a class of vessels known popularly as "Ninety-Day Gunboats" because they were built quickly of unseasoned wood. Ordered as a stop-gap measure by the U.S. Navy, these ships sailed well but rolled heavily. Involved in passage of forts Jackson and St. Philip and combat with CSN vessels, April 24, 1862. Involved in capture of Galveston October 4, 1862, and Battle of Galveston January 1, 1863. Returned to Galveston January 10, then patrolled Gulf Coast. Served with expedition to Brazos Santiago, Texas, October 27–November 3, 1863. Patrolled Gulf Coast until war's end. Decommissioned July 12, 1865, sold October 25, 1865. Sailed as merchant ship *Lulu* until at least 1885. Captured twelve prizes.

U.S.S. *Rachel Seaman*
Two masted schooner rigged sailing vessel
(launched 1861, acquired September 21, 1861)

Dimensions: 303 tons, 115' length, 30' beam, 9' draft.
Crew: 13
Armament (Sept. 1862): 1x 32pd SB; 1x 12pd R

War record: Privately owned vessel bought by the navy for blockade service. Considered a poor sailer and was often in for repairs. Patrolled the Gulf Coast for its entire martial career, aiding in the reduction of the Confederate position at Sabine Pass, September 25, 1862. Captured six vessels before being decommissioned and sold in May 1865.

U.S.S. *Sachem*
Small screw combatant
(launched 1844, acquired September 20, 1861)

Dimensions: 197 tons, 121' length, 23' 6" beam, 7' 6" draft.
Crew: 52
Armament (Jan 1863): 4x 32pd SB, 1x 20pd Parrot R

War record: This aging wooden hulled screw schooner served its entire military career in the Gulf and Mississippi, serving as the scout and survey vessel for the bombardment of forts Jackson and St. Philip in April 1862. Served as blockader off Texas, engaging Rebel batteries at Aransas Pass in June. Pulled into Galveston, Texas, in December,

1862 for boiler repairs and was on hand and sustained damage during Battle of Galveston on January 1, 1863. Disabled by Confederate gunners at Sabine Pass on September 8, 1863, and captured. Never sailed again.

U.S.S. *Sciota*
Screw gunboat, two mast schooner rigged.
(launched October 15, 1861, commissioned December 15, 1862)

Dimensions: 691 tons, 158' 4" length, 28' beam, 9' 6" draft.
Speed: 10 knots
Crew: 114
Armament (Jan 1863): 1x XI-inch Dahlgren; 2x 24pd SB; 1x 20pd Parrot R

War record: Belonged to a class of vessels known popularly as "Ninety-Day Gunboats" because they were built quickly of unseasoned wood. Ordered as a stop-gap measure by the U.S. Navy, these ships sailed well but rolled heavily. Involved in passage of forts Jackson and St. Philip and combat with CSN vessels, April 24, 1862; bombardment of Grand Gulf, Mississippi, June 9–10, passed Vicksburg June 28. Engaged C.S.S. *Arkansas*, July 15, 1862. Involved in operations below Donaldsonville, Louisiana October 4, 1862. Engaged in bombardment of Galveston January 10, 1863 and patrolled Texas Coast. Sank after collision with U.S.S. *Antona* in lower Mississippi River, July 14, 1863. Raised and refitted in August U.S.S. *Sciota* returned to Texas in December 1863 with Banks's expedition. The ship struck a mine near Mobile, Alabama, April 14, 1865 and sank. The vessel was raised, salvaged, and sold later that year. Sailed as merchant *Poncas* until sold to Chile as gunboat *Nubie*. *Sciota* captured or destroyed eight Rebel merchants.

U.S.S. *Velocity*
Small Schooner
(acquired September 30, 1862)

Dimensions: 87 tons
Crew: 12?
Armament (Jan 1863): 1x 24pd How

War record: Small blockade runner captured by U.S.S. *Kensington* and U.S.S. *Rachel Seaman* off Sabine Pass, September 25, 1862. Served off of Texas coast before being recaptured on January 23, 1863. Captured one prize.

U.S.S. *Westfield*
Ex-Ferryboats-4th Rate Side-wheel combatant
(launched 1861, commissioned December 2, 1861)

Dimensions: 891 tons, 215' length, 35' beam, 13' 6" draft.
Crew: 116
Armament (Jan 1863): 1x IX-inch Dahlgren; 4x eight-inch SB; 1x 100pd Parrot R

War record: New York Harbor ferryboats made excellent gunboats because of their agile maneuverability and their strengthened decks were capable of carrying heavy guns. U.S.S. *Westfield* participated in the passage of forts Jackson and St. Philip and the fight with the CSN vessels on April 24, 1862. Later, it fought at Vicksburg on June 26–28. *Westfield*, as flagship of Commodore William Renshaw's flotilla, next went to Texas where it participated in the capture of Galveston on October 4, 1862 and the bombardment of Port Lavaca on October 31–November 1, 1862. Aground during the disaster at Galveston on January 1, 1863, the vessel was scuttled to prevent its capture.

Other Union Vessels
Steamer *Saxon*
Steamer *Mary A. Boardman*
Steamer *Cambria*
Supply ship *Cavallo*
Supply ship *Elias Pike*

FURTHER READING

Barr, Alwyn. "Sabine Pass, September, 1863." Texas Military History (February, 1962), 17–22.

_____. "Texas Coastal Defense, 1861–1865." *Southwestern Historical Quarterly* 65 (1961), 1–31. This important work emphasizes the problems of defending the Texas coast during the War for Southern Independence as well as some of the innovative solutions.

Bosson, Charles P. *History of the Forty-Second Regiment Infantry, Massachusetts Volunteers.* Boston: Mills, Knight and Company, 1886. This book contains one of the best accounts of the Battle of Galveston.

C.S.A. Prize Commission. *In the Matter of the Confederate States of America vs. the Gunboat Steamship called the "Harriet Lane."* The proceedings of the commission reveal details and contain accounts of the Battle of Galveston of paramount importance. Available at the Local History Section, Rosenberg Library, Galveston, Texas.

Cumberland, Charles C. "The Confederate Loss and Recapture of Galveston, 1862–1863." *Southwestern Historical Quarterly* 51 (1947), 109–130. This article draws mostly from reports in the *Official Records.*

Darst, Maury. "Artillery Defenses of Galveston, 1863." *Military History of Texas and the Southwest* 12 (1975), 63–67.

Day, James M. "Leon Smith: Confederate Mariner." *East Texas Historical Journal* 3 (March 1965), 34-49.

Duganne, A.J.H. *Camps and Prisons: Twenty Months in the Department of the Gulf.* New York: J.P. Robens, 1865. An excellent, though hard-to-find book. Duganne was a historian turned Union colonel. After his capture in Louisiana, he was interned with the prisoners taken from Galveston and

Sabine Pass. Based on conversations with them, including Isaac Burrell, he writes a fascinating account of the fights.

Ellis, Louis Tuffly. "Maritime Commerce on the Far Western Gulf, 1861–1865." *Southwestern Historical Quarterly* 77 (1973). An important source for information on blockade running from Texas ports.

Evans, Clement, ed. *Confederate Military History: Library of Confederate States History in Twelve Volumes Written by Distinguished Men of the South.* 12 vols.; Atlanta: Confederate Publishing Co., 1899. Volume 11 deals with Texas.

Fitzhugh, Lester N. "Saluria, Fort Esparanza, and Military Operations on the Texas Coast, 1861–1864." *Southwestern Historical Quarterly* 61 (1957), 66–100.

Franklin, Robert M. "Speech to Camp Magruder United Confederate Veterans, April 2, 1911." Texas and Local History Collection, Rosenberg Library, Galveston, Texas. This pamphlet is an excellent primary account of the battle.

Frazier, Donald S. *Blood and Treasure: Confederate Empire in the Southwest.* College Station: Texas A&M University Press, 1995. An account of Sibley's invasion of New Mexico with good information about many of the men who fought at Galveston and Sabine Pass.

_____. "Cottonclads in a Storm of Iron." *Naval History* 8 (1994): 26–32. A general overview of the battle of Galveston.

_____. "Sibley's Brigade at the Battle of Galveston." *Southwestern Historical Quarterly* 99 (1995) 175–198. This article is the latest and most comprehensive scholarship on the subject.

Freeman, Douglas Southall. *Lee's Lieutenants.* 3 vols. New York: Charles Scribner's Sons, 1944. Still the best source for biographical information on officers who served in Virginia, including Magruder.

Garner, Ruby Lee. "Galveston During the Civil War." M.A. thesis, University of Texas, Austin, 1927. An early telling of the Galveston story, this work includes information about the city before and after the battle.

Gary, Cartwright. *Galveston: A History of the Island.* New York: Atheneum, 1991. A book by a popular writer. Beware of historical errors while reading its well-written prose. Best used as a general introduction to the city—very little on the battle.

Goyne, Minetta Altgelt. *Lone Star and Double Eagle: Civil War Letters of a German-Texas Family.* Fort Worth: Texas Christian University Press, 1982. An excellent primary account of a Texas coast watcher company.

Hall, Martin Hardwick. *The Confederate Army of New Mexico.* Austin, Tex.: Presidial Press, 1978. The absolute best source for muster roll and biographical information on Sibley's Brigade prior to 1863.

Hayes, Charles W. *Galveston: History of the Island and the City.* 2 vols. Austin, Tex.: Jenkins Garrett Press, 1974. The best work on the history of Galveston to 1900. Because of some mishap, the original book was not published when finished near the turn of the twentieth century. It took the intervention of publishers in the 1970s to resurrect this excellent work.

Hooverstol, Paeder Joel. "Galveston in the Civil War." M.A. thesis, University of Houston, 1950. A limited improvement on Ruby Lee Garner's thesis.

McComb, David G. *Galveston: A History.* (Austin, Tex.: University of Texas Press, 1986). A general survey of the city.

Marvin, David P. "The Harriet Lane." *Southwestern Historical Quarterly* 39 (1935). An excellent biography of a ship.

Muir, Andrew Forest. "Dick Dowling and the Battle of Sabine Pass." *Civil War History* 4 (1958), 399–428. One of the most comprehensive articles on Sabine Pass.

Naval Historical Center, Department of the Navy, *Dictionary of American Fighting Ships.* 8 vols. Washington: Government Printing Office, 1975–1981. A good starting point for information on Civil War naval combatants.

Noel, Theophilus. *A Campaign From Santa Fe to the Mississippi: Being a History of the Old Sibley Brigade From Its First Organization to the Present Time; Its Campaigns in New Mexico, Arizona, Texas, Louisiana and Arkansas in the Years 1861-2-3-4.* Edited by Martin Hardwick Hall and Edwin Adams Davis. Houston, Tex.: Stagecoach Press, 1961. The most recent edition of an excellent history of Sibley's Brigade written by a participant.

Price, Marcus W. "Ships that Tested the Bloackade of the Gulf Ports, 1861–1865." *American Neptune* 12 (1952), 154–236.

Sandefur, H. L., and Archie P. McDonald. "Sabine Pass: David and Goliath." *Texana* 7 (1969), 177–188.

Sifakis, Stewart. *Compendium of the Confederate Armies, Texas.* New York: Facts on File, 1995. A useful listing of all Texas units.

Silverstone, Paul H. *Warships of the Civil War Navies.* Annapolis, Md.: United States Naval Institute Press, 1989. The best collection of photographs and ship information in print.

Simpson, Harold B. "The Battle of Sabine Pass." In *Battles of Texas.* Waco: Texian Press, 1967.

Spell, Timothy. "John Bankhead Magruder: Defender of the Texas Coast." M.A. Thesis: Lamar University, 1981. A useful biography of "Prince John."

Tolbert, Frank X. *Dick Dowling at Sabine Pass.* New York: McGraw Hill, 1962. A colorfully told account of the battle.

Trexler, H. A. "The Harriet Lane and the Blockade of Galveston." *Southwestern Historical Quarterly* 35 (1931). A look at the problems caused to the Federal Navy by the capture of the Harriet Lane.

Williams, Edward B. *Rebel Brothers: The Civil War Letters of the Truehearts*. College Station: Texas A&M Press, 1995. The published letters of two Galveston brothers. Although most of the letters were written from distant battlefields to the folks back home, there is important correspondence concerning the Battle of Galveston.

Wooster, Ralph. *Texas and Texans in the Civil War*. Austin, Tex.: Eakin Press, 1995. A valuable survey of Texas during the war, including the various coastal engagements.

Wright, Marcus J. *Texas in the War, 1861–1865*, edited by Harold B. Simpson. Hillsboro, Tex.: Hill Junior College Press, 1965. Poorly organized, but so far the only work in print that lists some of the more obscure units and officers involved.

Young, Jo. "The Battle of Sabine Pass." *Southwestern Historical Quarterly* 52 (1949).

PHOTO CREDITS

We are grateful to the United States Army Military History Institute, Carlisle Barracks, Pennsylvania, for photographs of Isaac S. Burrell, Frederick Crocker, Edmund J. Davis, David G. Farragut, John Guest, Richard L. Law, John N. Maffit, John B. Magruder, William B. Renshaw, Raphael Semmes, and J.M. Wainwright.

We thank the Harold B. Simpson Confederate Research Center, Hillsboro, Texas, for permission to reproduce photographs of Arthur P. Bagby, Xavier B. Debray, James Reily, and William Read Scurry.

For the picture of Thomas Green we credit Archives Division, Texas State Library, Austin, Texas.

For permission to use photographs of Leon Smith and a drawing of the Battle of Galveston we are grateful to the Rosenberg Library, Galveston, Texas.

Photographs of the U.S.S. *Harriet Lane*, the U.S.S. *Brooklyn*, and the capture of the *Harriet Lane* were taken from David Porter's *The Naval History of the Civil War* (New York: Sherman Publishing, 1886).

We credit the U.S. Navy Imaging Center for the picture of the sinking of the U.S.S. *Hatteras*.

The photograph of the C.S.S. *Florida* was taken from the *Official Records of the Union and Confederate Navies*, Series I, Volume I.

INDEX